Rise and Fight
Speeches from the 1943-1945 Italian Social Republic, and the "Political
Testament"

Benito Mussolini

Speeches from the 1943-1945
Italian Social Republic, and
the "Political Testament"

First edition, first printing 2025.
Translated by Michael Joseph.
Cover art by Swifty.
Edited by Tom Simpson.
Layout by Louis Condé.

Antelope Hill Publishing | antelopehillpublishing.com

Paperback ISBN-13: 979-8-89252-049-2
EPUB ISBN-13: 979-8-89252-050-8

Table of Contents

Translator's Note:

Throughout the text, I have noted discrepancies between *Risorgere e Combattere* (RC) and the authoritative collected works of Mussolini, *Opera Omnia* (OO). Most of these discrepancies are transcription errors, and my notes are intended to explain any divergence from the text of RC. In most cases, especially where I simply note an error in the text, these notes are not intended for readers.

I have copied RC's unusual, and in my view, necessary formatting for the Political Testament. Many of the remarks by Cabella, Mussolini's interviewer, are absent from the version published in OO, and if I am not mistaken, they have never appeared in English.

RC—*Risorgere e Combattere*—*Rise and Fight*

OO—*Opera Omnia*, Volume XXXII (La Fenice, Florence, 1960). *Opera Omnia* is the definitive thirty-five-volume collected works of Mussolini, published by La Fenice from 1951 to 1962.

TN—Translator's Note. All notes *not* marked [TN.] are notes in the original text (RC).

Preface

Italy's collapse in the summer of 1943 was first political, then military. The settling of scores on July 25th, completely internal to Fascism, when the Grand Council voted no confidence in Mussolini, as if it were any old democratic parliament, was the moment that the faithless king and his Masonic, Anglophile court were waiting for to rid themselves of Il Duce, to suffocate the regime, and to throw themselves into the arms of the enemy. As for Germany, which was doggedly defending our territory from the invading Allies, this was the consummation of the blackest of betrayals.

The conspiracy of July 25th, and the ruinous unconditional surrender of September 8th, were events that demonstrated the inner weakness of the regime at that juncture, as well as the poor penetration of Fascism, not of course within the masses, but within the Italian ruling class, who had, after so many years, very often remained essentially liberal and reactionary. Corroded not so much by three years of war, which brought so much darkness, but also occasional light, in the struggle against the Anglo-American superpower, as by the clandestine activity of an entire formation of conservative power, Fascism was defeated by its internal enemies before it was defeated by its external enemies. From the Army General Staff to the Crown, from the Vatican to the major capitalist interests, all were agreed on sabotaging the war and the regime in exchange for a badge of honor from the western powers. The power of the enemies of Fascism was revealed in the summer of 1943, after twenty years of suppression. This was the summer of betrayal, of dishonorable defeat, of the "death of the Fatherland."

The cluster of conspiracy, compromise, and cowardice that led to the coup d'état of July 25th, and then to the dissolution of the state structure, by way of the most humiliating peace in the history of Italy, was formed by the convergence of many factors. Among these, the breakdown of the Italian Fascist Party, held by a weak hand at a crucial moment, played an important role. As did Mussolini's mysterious lack of resolve, after sliding into apathy following the ignominious fall of Pantelleria. These factors, along with the population's war fatigue (bombardments, food shortages, etc.), coalesced into the murky plot of the conspirators, and created the preconditions for catastrophe.

If September 8th meant the collapse of the state, the abandonment of the army, and the unraveling of the social fabric, that dreadful date is also and above all remembered by history as a triumph of the monarchy's cowardice: the king, a fugitive in the night, and his entourage of criminal generals, faithless officials, and anti-fascist relics dug from their grave after twenty years of sheepish silence.

Counterbalancing this day of humiliation, the following September 12th—the day of Mussolini's liberation from Badoglian imprisonment on Gran Sasso—provided the first sign of recovery. Even if, here and there, there were fascists who had already reopened headquarters and gathered their men, this date, along with the certainty that Il Duce would launch a new program founded on the authentic revolutionary principles of Fascism, unleashed a new enthusiasm, which would lead to many tens of thousands of Italians subscribing to the new Republican Fascist Party over the next few months.

In a climate as harsh and dramatic as few others in history, the Italian Social Republic was built by just a handful of men.

There is no need to retell the story of this one-of-a-kind, historic experience. It is hard to find another such case, not just in Italy, but in world history: a political movement at the helm of a sovereign state, embroiled in a war that seemed to promise only defeat, universally judged to be on the verge of a bloody resolution, but nevertheless enlisting hundreds of thousands in terms of volunteer fighters, institutional participation, and support for a leader who, up until the last weeks of his life, aroused a passionate popular consensus (as was demonstrated by his visit to Milan in December 1944). This latter phenomenon was the most incredible, given how the Anglo-Americans were then stationed only a few miles from Bologna.

In any case, it must be said that the Social Republic was a rebellion—political and ideological, but also military, emerging from a vanguard, a minority—against the surrender of the lower and upper bourgeoisie. This minority managed to act as a binding factor for society, and obtain material results through the work of the government (stabilizing prices, advanced social legislation, balancing the budget, etc.)[1] and the people (voluntary military and civil service,

---

[1] On the successes of the economic and social policies of the Italian Social Republic (RSI), see for example, Riccardo Lazzeri, *Economia e finanza nella Repubblica Sociale Italiana* (1943–1945), Ed. Terziaria-ASEFI, Milan 1998. Anti-fascist historiography also recognizes these achievements: cf. Silvio Bertoldi, *Salò. Vita e morte della Repubblica Sociale Italiana*, Rizzoli, Milan 1976. On page 314, for example, the author writes of the RSI's Finance Minister Domenico Pellegrini Giampietro: "It must be acknowledged that he governed better in the North, despite immense difficulties, than his counterpart in the Badoglio

mobilization of women in the auxiliary corps as well as armed units, social solidarity, etc.), results that were truly sensational if we take into account the tragic historical period.[2] More generally, it can be said that with the RSI there was a ferocious, desperate effort to stem the moral and material annihilation wrought upon an entire nation by the monarcho-plutocratic plot.

As Mussolini affirmed on September 27th, 1943 at the first meeting of the Republican Council of Ministers in the Rocca delle Caminate: "Though savagely tormented by Anglo-American bombardments," Italy on July 25th "was, apart from western Sicily, intact as a state and territory." He continues:

> The tricolor was still flying high in Rhodes, in Tirana, in Ljubljana, in Split, in Corsica, on the Var. Today, two months later, the enemy occupies a third of the national territory, and all of our positions beyond the national territory and overseas have been cleared. The loss of these positions, though they had cost the Italian people

---

government did in the South: it is possible that he found more understanding from a person like Rahn, than the legitimate government found among the allies in Salerno and Rome." This observation, by itself, refutes many of the anti-fascist assumptions about the subordination of Italians to the Germans during the RSI.

[2] For example, in early 1944, Pino Romualdi, deputy secretary of the Republican Fascist Party (PFR),·counted "more than two hundred thousand youngsters who came to our barracks as volunteers, and some who were already on the frontline" (*Fascismo repubblicano* [1945], Sugarco Edizioni, Milan 1992, p. 56). Another revealing data point shows that on July 31st, 1944, within the territory controlled by the RSI, there were around forty thousand women in the Fascist Republican Women's Groups (cf. Roberto D'Angeli, *Storia del Partito Fascista Repubblicano*, Castelvecchi, Rome 2016, p. 93).

so much blood and sacrifice, was provoked by the
harshest of armistices, the likes of which history
has never before witnessed, concluded behind the
backs of Italy's allies, and thus involving an
unprecedented betrayal, which was enough to
forever dishonor the monarchy and its
accomplices. The consequences of the armistice
were simply catastrophic: the consignment of the
Italian Navy to the enemy, the humiliating
liquidation of all other Italian military forces via
disarmament, the persistent, ruthless
bombardment, which continued during the
ongoing negotiations until early August, the
slaughter of the national soul, the spiritual and
material disorder, the continuation of the war on
our territory, as anyone could have predicted.[3]

Clearly, this was not just a matter of geopolitics. It is certainly true that
Italy, accepting unconditional surrender at a time when the war as a
whole was anything but lost, saw its geopolitical influence crumble in
an instant, to a degree not seen since Ancient Rome.[4] But the worst of

---

[3] Benito Mussolini, *Opera Omnia*, edited by Edoardo and Duilio Susmel [1960],
La Fenice, Florence-Rome 1983, vol. XXXII, pp. 6–7
[4] As attested by historical documentation, the day after the Battle of Stalingrad
ended (February 1943), the German positions were still such that Stalin made a
major diplomatic effort to reach a separate peace agreement with the Third
Reich. Cf. Elena Aga Rossi, *Una nazione allo sbando. L'armistizio italiano del
settembre 1943*, Il Mulino, Bologna 1993, pp. 32–33, where it is claimed that, in
contrast with Roosevelt's intention to require "unconditional surrender," 1943
"was the period in which the Soviets were putting major effort, with a series of
advances toward the German leadership, into a separate peace." It should also

it was that Italy had in that moment lost its soul, along with its centuries-old personality, and the Italian people were no longer the same. There was, as much among the masses as among the upper echelons—and in particular among those intellectuals who would set the tone of the coming decades—a kind of decay of character, a genuine ethical collapse that was also anthropological. Merging with the self-importance of two eternally foreign and therefore hostile influences (Catholicism and the parties of the "left," from the Risorgimento onward, forever enemies of Italian tradition and destiny), this was the basis of the crumbling of national-popular feeling in the consciousness of Italians.[5] This was a sentiment that had been tirelessly and bloodily constructed in only a few years, beginning with the taking of Libya in 1912, and continuing with the Great War, the Fiume enterprise, the March on Rome, the colonial war of 1935–36, and finally the wars of Spain and 1940.

With Fascism, the national idea reached its maximum and most complete Italian realization. Through Fascism, the "nationalization of the masses" found its form. Such admission of the masses into the

---

be noted that Italy's setbacks, following the Anglo-American landing in Sicily, and German fears of imminent Italian collapse, led to Germany's failure in the Battle of Kursk (Operation Citadel) in July 1943. Cf. Alan Bullock, *Hitler and Stalin*, New York, Knopf 1992, p. 871: "If Citadel had been carried out in May 1943, as originally intended, it might have succeeded; but, when May came, Hitler was confronted with a major threat in Italy. Citadel had to be postponed." The absence of a military solution in the east, as we know, was one of the factors that accelerated contact among the conspirators of July 25th: the monarch, the military caste, disloyal superiors, upper-class capitalists, the Vatican. On the participation of the latter in the plot to depose Mussolini and achieve surrender, see Ruggero Zangrandi, *1943: 25 luglio–8 settembre*, Feltrinelli, Milan 1964, p. 43.

[5] Editor's note: To say that Catholicism is foreign to Italy of all places is highly questionable. This is likely just a derogatory remark.

State had never even been attempted by pre-fascist, liberal Italy, which had remained an oligarchic and reactionary structure. In this sense, fascist authoritarianism, which arose from contingencies more than ideological commitments, was seen as an occasion for the kind of political growth and maturation of the Italian people that had never before been tried by any government.[6]

As has already been well stated,

> [t]he decline of our national identity began with the foundation of post-fascist democracy, partly as a consequence of the fact that political hegemony was then seized by forces, such as the parties of the left and the Catholic party, which received their legitimation from beyond the borders of the Nation.[7]

This gradual exhaustion of Italian identity, consummated in the climate of reluctance and disavowal that led to the orgy of betrayal in the summer of 1943, had disastrous historical consequences. The results can still be easily verified today, by observing the appalling, suicidal absence of national dignity and communal identity evidenced by the substantial minorities that lead our people. These minorities, steeped in Catholic and Enlightenment universalism, and imbued with

---

[6] Cf. Roberto Chiarini, *L'ultimo Fascismo. Storia e memoria della Repubblica*, Marsilio, Venice 2009, p. 28: "In the end, Fascism, with its intention to integrate the masses into the State, did nothing more than try to popularize, and give a strongly authoritarian twist to, the idea of the Nation, which since the Risorgimento had constituted the only true, strong collective idea of Italians sticking together."

[7] Elena Aga Rossi, op. cit. p.160.

inexhaustible hatred for anything touched by Italian and European cultural tradition, have, since the democratic and anti-fascist restoration of 1945, worked tirelessly against the interests of the people, and—as we see so clearly today—have managed to program the demolition of the national Fatherland and the ethno-anthropological fabric of Italian society that goes back three millennia.

The welding of Catholicism to the forces of the "left" (which have meanwhile passed from Marxism to liberal-democratic radicalism) is a sinister phenomenon that has revealed a pathological hostility toward every element of Italianity, and is rooted in the betrayal of 1943. The collapse of Italian character, which was already at work within our imperfect national unity, was encouraged by the self-inflicted defeat of Fascism on July 25th, and reached its finale with the ignominious surrender of September 8th 1943, with lethal, historic consequences for the Italian people.

Despite this context of genuine horror, the RSI represented above all a will to fight and revolt, right when all the worst elements of the surviving pre-fascist Italian bourgeoisie were zealously serving the interests of the Anglo-Americans, and irreversibly undermining the Nation as the fate of future ages was being decided. But the new Republic was also a political and social laboratory. With courage and tenacity, an effort was undertaken to construct a more just and advanced civilization of labor, giving life to a people's state founded on corporate solidarity, thus returning to the postulates of the original conception of Fascism.[8] As Mussolini himself repeatedly made clear,

---

[8] Concerning Mussolini's fresh desire, after being liberated, to work toward the "creation of a new government and a new party," and thus to return to an active political life, refuting what is still said about Germany exerting pressure on a

beginning with his first speech on Radio Munich on September 18th, 1943: "The state that we want to establish will be national and social in the highest sense of those words; namely, it will return to the fascism of our origins."[9]

In summary, it was on a terrain of enormous upheavals, and right in the middle of the most destructive of wars, that Mussolini, returning to the political stage after his liberation by German paratroopers from Campo Imperatore, committed his last and most dramatic revolutionary act with the Italian Social Republic.

Even in his first rallying call, Mussolini clarifies certain points that would remain central to the political design of the RSI. The establishment of a true social state took top position in Il Duce's plan to resume the revolution, now that the monarchy, the Vatican, and major capitalist interests, lining up behind the enemies of Fascism, had relieved him of their burden, after having slowed down or directly sabotaged the previous revolutionary program of the Sansepolcrists for twenty years. Echoing the ideological watchwords of the early days, the annihilation of the parasitic plutocracy that was governing the world (no less than it does today), and the final struggle against usurious capitalism in the name of the rising labor state, was the practical side of the traditional fascist calling to liberate the people from enslavement by private interests. Il Duce's appeal during the historic radio speech of September 18th helps us to understand the

---

tired and compliant Duce, see the first-hand testimony of Otto Skorzeny, with whom Mussolini spoke during the flight from Vienna to Munich on September 13th. Cf. Otto Skorzeny, *Vivere pericolosamente* [1970], Edizioni Settimo Sigillo, Rome 2019, p. 221.

[9] The speech delivered on Radio Munich on the evening of September 18th, 1943, was published the next day in *Corriere della Sera*.

foundation on which the new state would stand. Here, Mussolini promises the nascent Republic to the *squadristi*, the youth, women, laborers, peasants, office workers: in short, the people. To this we can add the extraordinary contribution of the intellectuals, who in surprising number joined the RSI, despite the perilous situation—in terms of personal safety too, as was made clear by the assassination of Gentile in a surprise attack by a group of *gappisti* in April 1944.[10]

From Marinetti to Pound, from Soffici to Comisso, from Primo Conti to Dainelli and Sironi, as well as many others, the RSI could count on the support of a cultural militancy that was entirely absent from the anti-fascist camp.

Behind the revolutionary radicalism of the RSI was a genuinely socialist impulse. Its social legislation was intended to pursue—after years of being merely "in favor of"—the creation of a people's state, which had been posited since the rise of the Fasci di Combattimento. In this, the Fascist Republic, with the accomplishments of socially oriented legislation, especially that of February 1944, was never less than crystal clear. Workers were released from the extortionate grips of employers, as well as the deceit of communist propaganda, as is evidenced by many of the figures and statements of the time.

For example, it was Fernando Mezzasoma, the RSI Minister of Popular Culture, who declared, in a speech from November 1944, that Italian workers:

---

[10] [TN.] Members of the *Gruppi di Azione Patriottica* (Patriotic Action Groups), small partisan groups formed in October 1943 that were aligned with the Italian Communist Party.

> have understood that by forging weapons they are
> forging the social future, founded on true socialism,
> on that socialism that must rise from the Italian
> people, if it is to survive, and not from the brains of
> American-brand capitalist speculators, or Marxist
> theorists inspired by the Moscow school.[11]

The dominant theme of social and socialist redemption of the Italian people was experienced as a myth, backed by intense ideological content that stretched back to the very foundations of the ongoing conflict. Back in 1940, it was defined by Mussolini as the war of proletarian countries against the wealthy countries of the west: recall the famous slogan, "blood against gold." This framing was renewed during the RSI, as a genuine "social war" that engaged the claims of the poor against those with a monopoly on the world's wealth. In the early twentieth century, Enrico Corradini prophesied a coming clash between the national socialism of European peoples and Anglo-American plutocratic imperialism, which would lead to international class war. Republican Fascism welded that revolutionary ideological heritage to another motive for total mobilization, which was launched by the Third Reich and taken up by the Social Republic, beginning with the eighteen points of the "Verona Manifesto": namely, the potent mythology of national and popular Europe in a struggle against a whole

---

[11] In Ermanno Amicucci, I 600 *giorni di Mussolini*, Editrice Faro, Rome 1948, p. 144. See also, among many others, Concetto Pettinato, *La Repubblica e i lavoratori*, an article that appeared in *La Stampa*, January 4th, 1944, republished in *Se ci sei batti un colpo. . . Cento articoli de La Stampa per la storia della RSI*, Editrice Lo Scarabeo, Bologna 2008, p. 71: "The real enemy is, for us as well as Russia, liberal capitalism, the regime of unlimited exploitation of labor and the unlimited profit of capital."

world of implacable enemies.

Point 8 of the November 1943 "Manifesto" penned in Verona hinges on foreign policy. After declaring the sacredness of the geographical and historical borders of Italy, the ultimate end of the war is described as the realization of a "European community" involving the federation of all nations that accept the following principles:

- Eliminating centuries-old British intrigues from our continent;
- Abolishing the internal capitalist system, and combating global plutocracy;
- Developing, to the benefit of the European and indigenous peoples, Africa's natural resources, while showing absolute respect for those peoples, especially the Muslims who, as in Egypt, are already civilly and nationally organized.[12]

For the first time in modern history, the project for a political community of the European peoples was taking shape in Italy. This was mirrored by ideas that were developing in National Socialist Germany at the same moment. Recall the 1943 document known as *Europa Charta*, by the economist Werner Daitz, theorist of large-scale economics,[13] in which he provided a programmatic structure for the "renaissance of Europe through European socialism," based on the

---

[12] Cf. Renzo De Felice, *Mussolini l'alleato, II, La guerra civile 1943–1945*, Einaudi, Turin 1997, pp. 610–613.
[13] [TN.] *Großraumwirtschaft*.

conception of Europe as a "family of peoples" united by a common bio-historical identity and common destiny.[14] This markedly ideological theme was among the most characteristic of the Social Republic, and constituted one of the main motives for those who fought for it. The ardent defense of Europe, a victim of the global assault of capitalism and communism united in conspiracy, was a central ideological pillar for the new political soldier.[15] It was in this context that the Republican Fascists determined that the ongoing war was a "war of civilization," fought in the name of the New Europe, through which would be realized the most complete form of fascism.

Besides politics and ideas, to look today at Mussolini's speeches of the last period of his long political militancy, namely the Social Republic, is to gain insight into history. According to the highest ethical principles, we recognize that, despite a military context that saw the prospects for victory and even self-defense gradually shrink, there was an Italian type that would never throw in the towel. Mussolini, having overcome the period of apathy which began with July 25th, was prepared to live the last revolutionary act with the energy of better times.

The determination to fight that existed on the ground, among the

---

[14] Cf. Various Authors, *Il Terzo Reich per l'Europa. La rivoluzione socialista europea* [1943–1944], Editrice Thule Italia, Rome 2012, from pp. 107 on.

[15] The propaganda of the RSI beat the drum of this European ideal, as was already noted among the international units of the Waffen-SS operating mainly on the eastern front. See for example, Luigi Canapini, *La repubblica delle camicie nere*, Garzanti, Milan 1999, p. 89, which cites a publication addressed to soldiers returning to Italy, after a period of training with the Germans: "[. . .] Our enemies have every reason to not want Europe to become a single and thus unbeatable bloc. You are a warrior for the new Europe that is cemented by the blood of fallen Europeans on the battlefields, thus realizing the prophecy of Giuseppe Mazzini."

National Republican Guard, the Black Brigades, La Decima, and among the volunteers in all military and civil sectors, was mirrored in the agitational discourse from the top. Il Duce had regained his charisma and his purpose, had recovered once more the role of *Capo*, the animating, magnetic pole of consciences. We often hear talk of a disheartened, pensive Mussolini, spending long months on Lake Garda. Perhaps this image is accurate. Certainly there were reasons for bitter reflection in his heart of hearts. But the political Mussolini, the man of action and ideas, is alive in the pages that follow. These pages remind us of the revolutionary *Capo*, still at the peak of his political vitality, a Mussolini who was fully aware not only of the dramatic nature of the historic moment, but also of the characteristic political and human will that was required to confront it.

This is where we get the measure of Mussolinian activism, where its ideal temperature is gauged: and it has to be especially high in the Social Republic. From the first speech of September 18th, 1943 to the last, brief and dramatic, delivered on April 23rd, 1945, in which Il Duce addresses the officers of the National Guard with spare, courageous words in the courtyard of the Milan Prefecture (from which would depart, two days later, the fatal convoy that would be stopped at Dongo). Between these two poles there lies the political and existential story not just of a man, however exceptional he may be, but of a whole people that would oppose with all its power a hostile destiny, in a fight that bore the hallmarks of a historically driven, vital energy.

These pages also testify to Mussolini's day-to-day commitment, exercised with a resolve that transcended the repeated setbacks that the last years had reserved for him. The anniversary of the Tripartite Pact; a gathering of auxiliaries; a visit to the men of the Resega; the emotional message on the fall of Rome on June 4th, 1944; the speech to the Muti Legionaries; the speech at the grave of D'Annunzio; the speech to the infantry of the Littorio Division training in Germany, where Mussolini spent several days among thousands of soldiers who saw in him the face of the Fatherland, and of which there remains exceptional film footage: all episodes of a larger story of valor, which was not only political. These episodes tell the story of a will to fight, and an inner resolve rarely seen in history.

The famous Lirico speech of December 16th, 1944 was delivered in an atmosphere of genuine enthusiasm, rendered all the more ardent by news from the western front, where the German offensive in the Ardennes appeared to have broken through American resistance, to open the way for further successes. Here, speaking of an Italy occupied by the Anglo-American enemies and their Badoglian servants, Mussolini affirms that "enemy oppression on the one hand, and the government's bestial persecution on the other, can only give more fuel to the movement of Fascism. Erasing the exterior symbols may have been easy, but suppressing the idea, impossible."

With seventy-four years of hindsight, we can only confirm how true this was. But the Lirico speech was also important, and especially so, for its conception of ideological continuity between the Social Republic and the Fascist regime, which traces a direct line back to the Sansepolcrist origins. Mussolini's affirmation of this continuity is highly important, given that, historiographically, it is often suggested that there was a break between the twenty-year regime and the RSI, which was not in fact the case. The Republic, simply put, impressed a new radicalism upon the revolution, which had been held back by conservative agents. The objectives of Fascism were always the same, in the principles of March 23rd, 1919, during the Fascist regime, and under the RSI.

At the Lirico, Mussolini put it clearly:

> Still and always calling ourselves fascists, and consecrating ourselves to the cause of Fascism, as we have done from 1919 to today, and will continue to do tomorrow, we have, after these events, beaten a new path of action, specifically in the political and social domains. More than a new path, we should more accurately say: a return to the original positions. It is historically documented that Fascism was, up to 1922, republican in tendency, and the reasons for which the 1922 insurrection spared the monarchy are well known.
>
> From the social perspective, the programme of republican Fascism is nothing but the logical continuation of the 1919 program, of the accomplishments of those wonderful years, from the Labour Charter to the conquest of the empire.

In his determination, there is a clear refutation of any suggestion that Il Duce was only republican in a minor sense, and that his republicanism was at the mercy of events. This detail is important, for it is among the elements that historically justify the existence of the RSI.

In any case, Goebbels himself, who was highly critical of Mussolini's submissiveness on July 25th, noted in his diary that at the Rastenburg headquarters Il Duce appeared "in splendid physical and mental condition. This can also be seen in the Orders of the Day, which are imbued with the old Revolutionary-Fascist spirit."[16] This authoritative testimony must be kept in mind, since it confirms that the speeches of the Social Republic that are republished here are delivered by a revolutionary *capo* at the peak of his dynamic power, and not by an aged political figure in decline, as is often insinuated.

Mussolini, up to the last days of the Republic, had faith in a turnaround. He repeatedly evoked, in Roman spirit, the fulfilment of a *fatum*, and never stopped believing that loyalty to an Idea was preferable to resignation. As we see so clearly from his words, he never gave up on inciting, on instilling energy and optimism, even in the face of imminent death. In fascist ethics, but also human ethics in general, a struggle is meaningful as long as the object for which one's passion is offered still lives. In this sense, we should recall the words of Mussolini's final speech: "If Italy were to die, our lives would not be worth living."

This was the mode of destiny and finality, the devotion to an Idea made manifest by a context of universal revolutionary war. This same extreme climate is found in another document presented here, the so-called *Political Testament* of Mussolini.

This is the account of a conversation that took place at the Milan Prefecture at Corso Monforte between Il Duce and the journalist Gian Gaetano Cabella on the afternoon of April 10th, 1945, the text of which was reviewed and signed by Mussolini himself two days later. Cabella was the director of Il *Popolo di Alessandria*, an uncompromising fascist

---

[16] Joseph Goebbels, *The Goebbels Diaries 1942–43*, Doubleday, New York 1948, p. 455.

newspaper that was among the most read during the RSI, with which Ezra Pound had collaborated. The testament also appears in summary and with some slight variations in Mussolini's *Opera Omnia*. It is therefore safe to assume its authenticity. In fact, it forms part of a series of informal testimonies through which Mussolini, especially in the later period of the Republic, intended to lay down precise statements concerning his current political thinking, in view of the historical context as well as the future. The text also reveals glimpses of Mussolini's humanity, precious for any biography of Mussolini during this period of extremity. The quality of this material is attested by Renzo De Felice himself,[17] who attributed full historical and political value to the conversation with Cabella.[18] Like other published conversations with Mussolini, the document entitled *Political Testament*, published for the first time in 1948 in Rome, proceeds almost like a Platonic dialogue. Thus, on April 20th, 1945, as the Führer's last birthday was being celebrated a thousand miles north in a surrounded bunker, Mussolini was setting out his positions. We'd like to highlight just one of these.

After reminding Cabella of the reasons for which Italy joined the war, Mussolini pinpoints, with the socialist revolutionary's gift for precision, the real and colossal stakes behind the Second World War. "Remember: we terrified the world of profiteers and speculators. They didn't want us to have any chance to live."

---

[17] [TN.] Italian historian (1929–1996) known for his authoritative, six-thousand-page biography of Mussolini.

[18] Cf. Renzo De Felice, op. cit. p. 59, where the conversation with Cabella is cited along with the other private political conversations that Mussolini had during that period with various figures: his son Vittorio, Carlo Silvestri (the old socialist who became close with Mussolini during the RSI), and Gioacchino Nicoletti, a republican fascist and scholar of Mazzini.

At the time when Mussolini was saying this, the partisan "resistance" was lavishly financed, as has been documented, by large Italian capitalist concentrations, such as the Banca Commerciale and Credito Italiano, but also Banca d'Italia, which had a hub for its anti-Italian plot at the Milan stock exchange. All these financial power centers offered their services to the systematic sabotage of the RSI's socializing legislation.[19] Mussolini adds another observation: "the worst thing is that our enemies have managed to get the proletariat, the poor, the neediest, to rally heart and soul behind those who starve them, the plutocrats of big capital."

Now more than ever, this grotesque paradox is alive and well. Now more than ever, the words of Mussolini grasp the burning actuality: at once denouncing oppression and spurring the mobilization necessary for any future awakening from the perverse cosmopolitan spell.

Luca Leonello Rimbotti[20]

---

[19] Cf. *ibid*, pp. 266–267.
[20] Luca Leonello Rimbotti has authored multiple books on fascism and has collaborated with the magazines has collaborated with the magazines *Elements*, *Italicum*, *Margini*, *Linea*, *Diorama Literary*, and *Trasgressioni*.

Benito Mussolini, just freed from Gran Sasso, poses with Otto Skorzeny near Campo Imperatore. It is September 12th, 1943: eleven days later—23 September—the Italian Social Republic will be born.

Speech Delivered on Radio Munich on the Evening of September 18th, 1943

Blackshirts, men and women of Italy!

After a long silence, my voice can once again reach you. I am sure you recognize it: it is the voice that has called you together in hard times and celebrated the Fatherland's triumphs with you.

I waited a few days before addressing you. After a period of moral isolation, I had to reacquaint myself with the world. Radio does not allow for long speeches. Leaving aside for now the prior circumstances, let us turn to the afternoon of July 25th, when the blackest adventure of my sufficiently adventurous life occurred.

My meeting with the King at Villa Savoia lasted twenty minutes at most. This was a man with whom all reasoning was impossible. He had already made his decision. Crisis was imminent.

In war or peace, a minister may resign, a commander may be ousted, but it is a unique occurrence in history when a man, such as the one who speaks to you now, who has served the King for twenty-one years with absolute—I repeat—absolute loyalty, is arrested at the threshold of the King's private residence, forced into a Red Cross ambulance on the pretext of saving him from a plot, and conducted headlong, first to one, and then to another carabinieri barracks.

My immediate impression was that this protection was in fact some form of detention. This impression only grew as I was conducted from Rome to Ponza. Then, with the journey from Ponza to Maddalena, and from Maddalena to Gran Sasso, I was finally convinced that the plan was to hand me over to the enemy.

Though I was completely isolated from the world, I had a strong feeling that the Führer was concerned for my fate. Goering sent me a telegram, more as a brother than as a comrade. Later, the Führer would have a truly monumental edition of Nietzsche's works sent to me.

The word "loyalty" has an unmistakable, deep significance, which I would say is eternal in the German soul. In both the collective and in the individual, this word sums up the German spiritual world.

I was convinced that I would see proof of this. Knowing the conditions of the armistice, I no longer had the slightest doubt about all that was hidden within Article 12. And besides, a senior official told me outright, "you are a hostage."

On September 11th, in the middle of the night, I was informed that the enemy would not let me live once they got their hands on me. In the limpid air of this imposing peak, there was a feeling of expectation. At 2:00 p.m. I saw the first glider land, followed by others. Squadrons of men were advancing toward the refuge, determined to smash through any resistance.

The guards watching over me understood what was happening, and did not fire a single shot. It lasted just five minutes. This feat of organization, of the Germanic spirit of decisiveness and initiative, will remain an unforgettable moment in the history of the war. With time it will become legendary.

So ends the chapter that might be called my personal drama. But this is a negligible episode compared to the terrifying tragedy into which the democratic, liberal, and constitutional government of July 25th has thrown the entire Nation. At first, I did not believe that the July 25th government would have such a disastrous plan for the Party, the Regime, and the Nation itself. But after several days, the first measures indicated that there was a plan underway that would destroy all the accomplishments of the Regime over the last twenty years, that would erase twenty years of glorious history that had given Italy an Empire and a standing on the world stage that it had never had before.

Today, before the ruins, before the ongoing war, some among us— we spectators on our own territory—may seek to split hairs and make room for compromise, or shift the blame, to prolong indecision.[21]

While we fully assume our own responsibilities, we want to make clear those of others, beginning with the Head of State.[22] Since he has not abdicated, as the majority of Italians had expected him to, we know now that he can and must be held responsible.

This same dynasty has been the principal agent of defeatism and anti-German propaganda throughout the whole war, despite the fact that the war was declared by the King himself. Their disinterest in the progress of the war, their prudent and not so prudent reserve, invited all the speculations of the enemy, while the heir to the throne,[23] who

---

[21] [TN.] Lines omitted from RC: "They split hairs about the new name of the Party. They are the same dead weight who have always slowed the march of the regime, and tried to sabotage its social achievements, and developments on the national and imperial level" (OO, 2).

[22] [TN.] King Vittorio Emanuele III.

[23] [TN.] Umberto II.

had intended to assume command of the armies of the south, never set foot on the battlefield.

I am now more convinced than ever that the house of Savoy willed, prepared, and organized the coup d'état, up to the finest details, with Badoglio as accomplice and executor, as well as certain gutless generals and cowardly elements of the Fascist Regime. There can be no doubt that immediately after my capture the King authorized the armistice negotiations, which had perhaps already begun between the dynasties of Rome and London.

It was the King who advised his accomplices to deceive the Germans in the most disgraceful manner, and denied that there were negotiations underway even after signing.

It was the whole dynastic complex that premeditated and executed the demolition of the Regime,[24] the same Regime that had in fact rescued it twenty years ago, and created the powerful internal diversion based on the return to the Statute of 1848, and protected freedom from the state of siege. As for the conditions of the armistice, which were supposed to be generous, they are the harshest in recorded history. The King of course made no objection to the premeditated delivery of my person to the enemy. By his actions, dictated by worries about the future of his Crown, it is the King who has created this chaotic and shameful situation for Italy, which can be summed up like so: in every continent, from the Far East to America, everyone now knows what honoring pacts means for the house of Savoy.

The same enemies, now that we have accepted a shameful

---

[24] [TN.] in *Opera Omnia*: "*fascismo*" (OO, 3).

capitulation, do not bother to hide their contempt. Nor could it be otherwise. The English, for example, who no one, especially not the Führer, ever conceived of attacking, entered the war, according to Churchill, because they had given their word to Poland.

From here on out, it may happen that even in private affairs Italians will be held in suspicion. If it were only the groups responsible that had to face the consequences, it would not be so bad. But do not deceive yourself: the price will be paid by the Italian people, from the first to the last citizen.

After our honor was compromised, besides the mainland territories occupied and sacked by the enemy, we also lost, perhaps permanently, all of our Adriatic, Ionian, Aegean, and French positions, which we conquered with no little sacrifice in blood. The Royal Army was rapidly and almost totally disbanded. There is nothing more humiliating than being disarmed by a betrayed ally, under the scorn of the local population.

The humiliation must have been especially cruel for those officers and soldiers who fought so bravely by the side of their German comrades on so many battlefields. The full weight of this shame must have been felt in those African and Russian cemeteries where Italian and German soldiers lie side by side.

The Royal Navy, built up entirely during the twenty years of fascism, has been consigned to the enemy in Malta, a country which constitutes, and will continue to constitute, a permanent menace to Italy, and the stronghold of English imperialism in the Mediterranean.

Only the air force was able to conserve a good portion of its equipment, but it, too, is practically disbanded. These are the indisputable facts, which the Führer, too, has documented, in the speech in which he relates hour by hour the deception of the Germans. This deception was only reinforced by the murderous bombardments of the large and small cities of central Italy, which the Anglo-Americans, in league with the Badoglio government, prolonged even after the armistice was signed.

Given these conditions, it is not the Regime that has betrayed the Monarchy, but the Monarchy that has betrayed the Regime, such that it has now lost its place in the minds of the people. It is simply absurd to suppose that this could even slightly compromise the unitary whole of the Italian people. When a monarchy fails in its duties, it loses all reason to exist. As for our traditions, they are more republican than monarchical: the unification and independence of Italy were wrought, against all the more or less foreign monarchies, by the republican current that had its pure and great apostle in Giuseppe Mazzini, more so than by the monarchists.

The state we intend to establish will be national and social in the broadest sense of these words: it will be a fascism that goes back to our origins. While our movement continues to develop its irrepressible force, our aims are the following:

> 1) Take up arms once more alongside Germany, Japan, and the other allies: only blood can erase such a shameful page of the Fatherland's history;
> 2) Prepare, without delay, the reorganization of our Armed Forces around the Militia formations; only those driven by a faith, who fight for a clear idea, have no need to measure sacrifice;

3) Eliminate the traitors, especially those who up to 9:30 p.m. on July 25th had fought, often for many years, in the ranks of the party, and have now entered the ranks of the enemy;

4) Annihilate the parasitic plutocracies and make labor, at last, the subject of the economy, and the unbreakable foundation of the state.

Loyal Blackshirts all over Italy!

I call you once more to work and to arms. The enemy's celebration of Italy's surrender does not mean that they have victory in their grips: the two great empires of Germany and Japan will never capitulate.

You, *squadristi*, rebuild the battalions that accomplished such heroic feats.

You, young Fascists, join the divisions that will repeat the glorious action of Bir el Gubi on the soil of the Fatherland.

You, aviators, return to your German comrades, to the cockpit, and make the enemy attacks on our cities a futile endeavor.

You, Fascist women, resume the work of moral and material support, essential to our people. Peasants, workers, and employees, the state that will emerge from this immense ordeal will be yours, and as such you will defend it against anyone who even dreams of reprisal. Our will, our courage, and your faith, will return to Italy its face, its future, its chance at life, and its standing in the world.

More than a hope, this has to be—for all of you—a supreme certainty.

Viva l'Italia!

Viva il Partito Fascista Repubblicano!

Message for the Anniversary of the Tripartite Pact, September 28th, 1943

I judge it a good sign that my return to Italy coincides with the anniversary of the Pact that indissolubly unites Fascist Italy, National-Socialist Germany, and the Empire of Japan.

The Fascist Republican Government is determined to fight with all its power, and with the confidence that has always inspired Italy, until ultimate victory.

Fascist republican Italy will wipe these days of humiliation from its history, and with its blood it will wipe away the shame that the degenerate Monarchy has tried to cast over the traditions and past glories of the country.

Together with the German and Japanese troops, the Italian Armed Forces will liberate the world from the international clique, which will not stop at betrayal to cast confusion among the Nations and their traditions.

Our German and Japanese comrades can rest assured that the Tripartite Pact will be respected by Fascist Republican Italy with the same determination and confidence that has inspired Italy over the last three years.

Mussolini in conversation with a young RSI volunteer.

Radio Message Broadcast December 11th, 1943 to Mark Japan's Entry into the War

The grave events of these last months, caused by the shameful capitulation perpetrated by the monarchy and its accomplices, have not altered the political stance of fascist republican Italy toward the other Powers of the Tripartite Pact.

On the anniversary of the signing of the Pact, the Government of the Italian Social Republic reaffirms in the most categorical and solemn manner its ideal and concrete solidarity with Germany and Japan.

Very soon this solidarity will have its most effective demonstration when the military forces that the Republic is swiftly preparing take up their combat positions alongside their Tripartite Pact comrades.

I can state with confidence that the armed forces of the Republic, driven by the will for reconquest that is radically renewed in the spirit and in the men, will erase with their struggle and their blood the dark page of betrayal and surrender. I am deeply convinced that these forces will be worthy of fighting alongside their German comrades, who have provided indisputable proof of valor on so many battlefields, and with the no less heroic soldiers of the Tenno, who have inflicted harsh defeats and scorching humiliations against America's Jewish plutocracy.

The continual air attacks against major and minor Italian cities, the heavy loss of innocent human life, the destruction of important monuments that were testaments to our creative power in the domains of the spirit, will not manage to bend the Italian people, but will rather spur their hatred and tenacity.

The leaders, the governments, the peoples of Germany and Japan, welcome my words with the same feeling that is summed up and dictated by these words: loyalty, camaraderie, faith that the long sacrifice will be crowned by victory.

Speech to the Regional Commanders of the Republican Army, January 30th, 1944

In light of the events that have followed, the unconditional surrender announced on the 8th of September, and signed on the 3rd, increasingly proves to be not only a deception of the Italian people, but a dreadful crime of *lèse patria*, and an act of reckless, suicidal insanity.

The consequence, easy to foresee, was the total demolition of all the Italian Armed Forces on land and sea, and in the skies. Demolition of personnel and materiel: in short, scorched earth. In late September, when we launched our reconstruction efforts—the contribution of Marshal Graziani, with the prestige he brings as a great soldier, should never be forgotten—there was literally nothing. The "moral" situation was perhaps worse than the dearth of material resources. I say this for the sake of certain generous though impatient people, who are ignorant of many things. We are back to the start, with arduous work ahead of us. Reconstructing a modern army is extremely difficult, especially in a country like Italy. The modern army of today is a technical-scientific organism. Artillery cannot be improvised: our artillery was deservedly famous for being, even with limited means, among the best in the world, and our Engineer Corps achieved advances that were recognized around the world.

The Army of the Italian Social Republic cannot and should not be a copy of what the Royal Army was. The leadership must be up to the task in both peace and in war. The obligation to abstain from any political activity does not imply indifference or agnosticism. The pledge of allegiance to the Republic signifies not only adherence to the new political form of the state, but to the totality of Fascist doctrine, which gives value, character, and historical content to the Republic: and all this, without the slightest private reservation.

No doors are left ajar. Once the oath is taken, all bridges are burned. It is a declaration of readiness to live and fight for the Republic. Exterior symbols are also important, as indicators of an explicit orientation. The salute, a show of discipline and hierarchy, will always be Roman; the stars will be replaced by a Roman sword adorned with branches of oak and laurel; the oath will be taken on February 9th, the 95th anniversary of the proclamation of the Roman Republic in 1849.

One problem prevails, which absorbs all the others. It also makes solving all the others more difficult. This problem is expressed in the categorical imperative to return to combat, to move from the status of war-martyr that currently defines Italy, with the destruction of its large and small cities, to a nation that wages war, where attack is met with attack.

The Anglo-American landing at Nettuno had a profound moral impact: it was a signal for the best Italians. Rome is a word of magical resonance. When the greatest among us cry "Rome or death," they mean that Rome is life, and thus history, and the heart of our race. For us, for you, it is a humiliation that burns—almost physically—the flesh: forced to be spectators of Rome's defense, entrusted for now to the unquestionable valor of the soldiers of the Reich. Any people with centuries of history has had to eat the bitter ashes of defeat at least once, only to return for revenge and a second shot. A nation incapable of such force of will exiles itself from history, and declares itself undeserving of bearing arms, the ultimate shame for any people worthy of the name. Do we want to inflict this undeserved and immense punishment on the hundreds of thousands of valiant men who have fallen in the name of Italy during thirty years of almost continuous war? I know the answer that throbs in your hearts.

There is only one command: prepare the men, the means, and, above all, the will, for the war effort of the months to come. Return to combat alongside our German allies, who have been carrying the entire weight of the European front so admirably. Only an army like that of Germany, reaching the fifth winter of the war—this war!—can fight, maneuver, and counterattack on fronts as immense as Russia, against numerically overwhelming forces, and turn the purely territorial advantages of Stalin's army into a costly problem. The truly exceptional offensive and defensive capabilities of the German forces are the result not only of the tactical and strategic intelligence of the leaders—universally recognized and no less universally documented— nor the quality of arms: it is also, and above all, the result of decisive moral factors, expressed in a strong national conscience and in the omnipresent sense of personal dignity. As for the German people—the so-called domestic front—they have shown what metal their souls are made of, which even incessant, massive bombardments have failed to bend, and will never bend.

As we wait—hopefully not for long—to see Italian soldiers alongside German soldiers on the battlefields once more, we must openly, sincerely, and cordially demonstrate to the German soldiers our camaraderie on a daily basis, which is the best preparation for the camaraderie of tomorrow, among the newly formed units, fighting for a common cause and destiny.

I thank you for what you have done up to this point, and for what you will do to restore the prestige, power, and future of a Nation without which, today or tomorrow, it is impossible to conceive of Europe.

While my words are addressed to your intellects, I think they have also touched the hearts of old and courageous soldiers.

Speech to the Sailors of San Marco in the German Training Camps, April 24th, 1944

Officers! Petty officers! Non-commissioned officers and sailors!

I bring you the Nation's greetings, along with the encouragement and good wishes of the Italian Social Republic. In the fifth year of this most arduous of wars, you have come to this great Nation, our friend and ally, which seems more iron-willed and uncompromising than ever, as if transformed into one giant workshop, a single barracks.

Here, men and women, old and young, work without watching the clock, while the soldiers who fight under the banner of the Führer furnish indelible proof of heroism in all the theaters of war, earning the respect of even their adversaries, and the admiration of the world.

You have come, and will remain for as long as it takes, to learn the modern methods of war, to learn the handling of many new and powerful weapons, to become soldiers in the fullest sense of the word, and to prepare, above all, the erasure of the shameful betrayal that was perpetrated not only against our ally, but first and foremost against the Italian people.

This shame will not be erased without resuming the fight against the invader who contaminates the sacred soil of the Fatherland.

Camped beyond the Garigliano are not only the cruel and cynical British, but also Americans, Frenchmen, Poles, Indians, South Africans, Canadians, Australians, New Zealanders, Moroccans, Senegalese, Negros and Bolsheviks. You will experience the joy of firing upon this mishmash of mercenary races, who respect nothing and no one in Italy.

Officers! Petty officers! Non-commissioned officers and sailors!

In the German training camps the foundation of the Italian Social Republic is being laid down. You have the singular privilege of participating in this new and great construction, and the highest honor of returning to combat.

The Fatherland depends on you in the certainty that your lion,[25] which once knew the triumphs of *la Serenissima*,[26] will soon, with spread wings, carry the sign of victory. *Viva l'Italia!*

---

[25] [TN.] The winged lion in the Piazza San Marco in Venice.
[26] [TN.] Venice ("the most serene").

Message Addressed to Italians on the Occasion of the Occupation of Rome, June 5th, 1944

Italians!

The Anglo-American invaders, for whom the monarchy's betrayal opened the doors of the Nation in Sicily and Salerno, have entered Rome. The news will deeply trouble you, as it does every one of us.

We do not intend, for the facile purposes of propaganda, to diminish the significance of this event, nor even emphasize the fact it was held back for so long, especially considering the lack of preparation. Step by step, with heroism that will remain imprinted in the memory of the population, the soldiers of the Reich contested every strip of Italian territory.

Out of respect for what the *Urbe* represents for world history and civilization, and to avoid inflicting an even harsher torment on a population already harshly tested by the siege, the German Command decided not to defend the city as it could have.

To Romans, we say this: do not morally yield to the invader, who brings within our walls the men of unconditional surrender, and a government dominated by an agent of Moscow.

To our brothers of Southern Italy, who have already suffered months of cruel and insulting Anglo-American oppression, we say: use every means at your disposal to make life difficult and dangerous for the invaders. To Italians in the provinces of the Italian Social Republic, we assure you that the fall of Rome does not diminish our energy, and even less our will to create the best conditions for reconquest. Every possible measure will be taken to this end, the fulfillment of which must dominate, imperiously, the consciences of all, whether in combat or in work.

To our allies of the Tripartite Pact, and in particular our German comrades, we reaffirm our unshakable determination to continue the struggle until victory. The word of the Republic is not like that of the King: only concerned with the fate of the Crown, and not that of the Country.

Soldiers, to arms! Workers and peasants, to work!
The Republic is under threat from the plutocracy and its mercenaries of every race. Defend yourselves!

Viva l'Italia! Viva la Repubblica Sociale Italiana!

Speech to the Monterosa Alpine Division in the German Training Camps, July 16th, 1944

Officers, petty officers, non-commissioned officers and soldiers of the Monterosa Alpine Division!

I promised your commander that I would visit your division. I have kept my word, and now I stand among you. Soon you will return to the Fatherland, and refute the foolish utterances, the criminal insinuations, that the friends of betrayal and the enemy's hired killers have spread about your departure for Germany.

You are the first large unit that returns to see the sky and the earth of the betrayed, divided, and tormented Fatherland. You are the main column of the temple, the cornerstone of the newly constructed Italian Armed Forces.

As Alpini, proud of your heroic traditions, proven in hundreds of battles, you deserve this exalted privilege, and as Alpini you undoubtedly appreciate the honor and responsibility that come with it.

Over the last months you have trained and refined your combat technique, under the guidance of instructors who have prepared some of the strongest soldiers in the world, as the enemy has been forced to recognize on numerous occasions.

Living among this great, allied people is enough to convince you that they merit victory, not only due to the power of their weapons, but above all due to their discipline and unbreakable spirit of sacrifice. Confident in my interpretation of your feelings, I want to thank the corps of instructors who have worked with and for you as comrades.

Upon your return to Italy, you can rest assured that on the frontline you will not be facing other Italians, be they simply misguided or genuine rebels. Along with a handful of Europeans, you will face people of Africa, Asia, and America: mercenaries with no ideals.

The spectacle that your division has offered me provides the utmost comfort. It is, and ought to, and will remain, a division of iron.

The Italy that Fascism gave the glories of the Empire—the Italy rescued from dishonor and betrayal by the Social Republic—considers you its best sons, and places all its hopes in you.

With irreproachable conduct prior to, during, and after combat, I am sure that you will not disappoint the hopes of the Fatherland, and will open the doors to liberation and victory.

July 1944. Sennelager, Germany, Il Duce visiting the Italian divisions in training.

Speech to the Italia Division Bersaglieri in the German Training Camps, July 17th, 1944

Officers, petty officers, non-commissioned officers, infantry of the Italy Division!

Your division has the great honor of bearing the immortal name of the Fatherland.

For more than a century, you have been, not only for the Italian people, but for all peoples, the symbol of the Italian Army. When you filed out to the blasts of your fanfare, the Italian people recognized themselves in you, and considered you the elect representatives of our race.

Today you have presented yourselves in a manner deserving of the highest praise. You have come to be trained in a friendly, allied country with glorious, centuries-old military traditions. You have all put yourselves on the line since the ill-fated 8th of September, when entire units rallied behind our German ally. You all understand the supreme necessity of taking up arms once again, to erase the page of September 8th in the only way possible: in combat.

Now that I have presented you with the banners of the Italian Social Republic, I ask you: are you ready to defend it with your blood?

I am confident that you will lead your division, which bears the name of Italy, toward reconquest.

Speech to the Sailors of the San Marco Division in the German Training Camps, July 18th, 1944

Officers, petty officers, non-commissioned officers, infantry of the San Marco Division!

Two months have passed since I had the great pleasure of meeting you and spending what was, for me, an unforgettable day with you. Since that day, further incidents have been visited upon our Nation. Rome, which in thirty centuries of history only saw Africans when they were chained behind the carriages of victorious Consuls, today has its walls profaned by these bastard, uncivilized races. While this must sadden you, it should also spur you on, toward the necessary reconquest.

You have presented yourselves in a manner that I can only describe as superb. In your conduct is visible not only the expression of your spirit and your will, but also the result of these months of training under the guidance of your German instructors. To these men I owe my gratitude. Above all, I want to draw attention to General Alberti, who has dedicated himself to you with particular attention and care.

You must feel like—you must be—an unbreakable block of heart and will. Soon you will have the pleasure of seeing the soil of the Fatherland once more.

I have presented you with the banners, and your division is therefore complete. These are the banners of the Italian Social Republic, around which the entire compact mass of working Italy are already converging.

These banners are the symbol of our faith, of our daring. I am certain that when the multicolored enemy of our Nation hears you cry *San Marco* they will realize they have fearless hearts before them, ready to give their all to seize victory.

Speech to the Infantry and Officers of the Littorio Division in the German Training Camps, July 18th, 1944

Officers, petty officers, non-commissioned officers, soldiers of the Littorio Division!

This visit brings to a close my cycle of inspections of the Italian Divisions that are preparing for reconquest in this allied, welcoming land.

Though all the divisions have presented themselves impeccably, yours, with the live-fire exercises that I've viewed, leaves me with the impression that your preparation is highly advanced, and that you have dedicated yourselves to your training with the necessary diligence, and the no less necessary enthusiasm.

In your presence, I want to thank General Von Hott, who oversees the training of the Italian Divisions in Germany, and General Von Tschudt, who has dedicated himself to your training with particular determination and energy. With Von Tschudt, I want to thank his collaborators, from the first to the last.

Your Division is called "Littorio" and it will keep that name. It is a name that has already been brilliantly consecrated during the wars in

Spain and in North Africa. It is a name that is particularly dear to us. It is under this symbol of the *littorio* that the legionaries of Ancient Rome marched and won.[27] It is the symbol of the Italian Social Republic.

More than a promise, it should elicit from your hearts a solemn oath. You will defend to the last drop of blood the banners that I am about to give to you. Never should it happen again that our German comrades, even for a day and only vaguely, come to regret having offered their modern weaponry for the reconquest of our Nation.

All of our spiritual and material energy must be aimed at this goal: rising up and fighting. The shameful betrayal and capitulation of September 8th will be erased in only one way: with blood. The motto I assign to your division is eternal and always relevant: "*All for one and one for all.* This is how the new and best destiny of the Nation will be prepared.

I will once again repeat, fellow officers, my satisfaction with the demonstration that I witnessed this morning. I paid close attention to the maneuver of the troops, as a whole and in detail. On this subject, it is not inappropriate to recall a phrase of Napoleon, who, needless to say, knew a thing or two about war: "There are no details; everything in military life is important. Even the movement of a soldier that might seem superfluous may be that that saves his life."

It is essential that you make the most of this training. Your teachers, as is clear to see, are unparalleled. There are specific weaknesses that must be overcome, though they may appear utterly trivial. You have to understand that the German people are an

---

[27] [TN.] The *fascio littorio*, or fasces.

eminently military people, who take things seriously, especially the most serious thing of all, which is war.

As for politics, our ideas have to be extremely precise. Above all, during a period of transition and crisis, mottos must have the timbre and hardness of metal.

On September 8th we experienced a historic episode that made us shudder with disgust and lower our heads. We have to realize the full scope of this episode, to understand what the current moment demands.

What happened was unheard of. Out of the blue, yesterday's ally, as our community of arms was still being exalted in the official bulletin, was abandoned in favor of the enemy. The Navy—the Navy that Fascism was entirely responsible for building, from the dreadnoughts to the small tugs—had no shame in consigning itself, guided by a half-Jew like Da Zara, to the enemy fleet in the port of Malta.

Faced with this ruinous spectacle, the task of reconstruction is not simple. The difficulties are in some cases exceptional. Nevertheless, day by day, these difficulties are being confronted; on German soil, the first divisions of the Italian Army are rising, and the Regiments to which they belong are being handed the banners of the Italian Social Republic. It is not only a Republic because the Italian tradition, including that of Piedmont, is more republican than monarchical, but also because, all of a sudden, we find ourselves with a monarchy that has dishonored itself with capitulation, and a king who, in an effort to save his own crown, simply joined the enemy. When such a thing occurs, it is time for systems and men to be liquidated.

Why "Social Republic?" For one obvious reason: the modern world has quite the collection of republics.

I hope that none of you intend to establish an ultra-parliamentary republic like that of France, drenched in Judaism and Freemasonry, nor a cantonized republic like that of Switzerland;[28] not to mention those overseas republics where "command" and "obedience" mean less with every change of season. It is clear that the Italian Social and Fascist Republic can only be inspired by the doctrine of Fascism and its teachings. Those who intend to remain undecided, and think they can camouflage themselves, are indulging in useless and cowardly calculation. Many of the traitors of yesterday have been punished, and others will be in the future.

The sufferings to which the Italian people have been subjected after September 8th may be described as unprecedented. The ones who in fact deserved this suffering were those who abandoned themselves on July 25th to the orgy of destruction of our symbols, in the belief that they could destroy what was indestructible: our works and spirit. And this suffering was deserved by those who, after September 8th, with almost unthinkable lack of awareness, sounded the bells, organized parades, lit bonfires on the mountains, on what was and ought to have been a day of the deepest national mourning. And so we have a false armistice, with clauses so crushing and draconian that still today, ten months later, no one has the courage to speak of them in public.

Now, violently, we must gather all the forces of our spirit that remain intact, and we must say: under such conditions, living is no longer important. Under these conditions, only one thing matters: fighting. He who does not fight today is a man who is already morally dead, or deserves to be.

---

[28] [TN.] A line was omitted from this sentence in RC: "a plutocratic republic like that of Roosevelt, or a communist one like that of Stalin." (OO, 104)

Comrades!

The memory of our meeting will, I believe, remain long in our hearts. We shall see each other again in Italy, when you will finally experience the joy of firing on the enemy who camps in the shadows of our ancient and universal monuments.

Thus we resume the battle to be a people again. For Italy has always faced this terrible dilemma: either it is great, or it ceases to exist.[29]

These weapons, comrades, have been given to you so that our ideals become reality.

---

[29] [TN.] "o è *grande o non è*," literally "either it is great, or it is not."

Speech for the Fourth Anniversary of the Tripartite Pact, September 27th, 1944

When the Tripartite Pact between Italy, Germany, and Japan was signed on September 27th, 1940, an act of historic importance was accomplished, considering what already appeared to be a fatal development in the ongoing war, and the decisive will of the Anglo-Saxons: global conflagration.

According to the understanding between the three allies, the Pact was also a intended as a warning, in the hope that the war could be prevented from propagating to continents that were still immune, and that confining the conflict might allow for a new organization of the world to emerge, based on the principle of international justice outlined in the preamble of the Pact itself, namely "that all nations of the world be given each its own proper place."

The Three-Power Pact was thus a defensive measure, in view of the plot that was already in the air,[30] that the so-called democratic nations were already weaving, to mortally wound the three great nations that represented the values and the form of the spirit,[31] hard work, and the

---

[30][TN.] *Complotto* ("plot") in OO, *compito* ("task") in RC.
[31] [TN.] *Forza* ("force") in OO, *forma* ("form") in RC.

right to peaceful expansion.

But besides being a defensive bond, the Tripartite Pact was also a pledge of solidarity and responsibility, to the great work that would give the world a new order, where the right to life of young people would be justly recognized, and the ancient injustices would be eliminated.

The pact was not signed for the sake of fleeting political contingencies. It was signed in harmony with the fatal logic of history, by the three peoples who, in Occident and Orient, were facing the supreme trial, and were, with their regimes of discipline and freely accepted sacrifice, the enunciators of a new era and a new way of life.

Subsequent events have only demonstrated how justified the nations were in their will to defend themselves against immiseration, at the hands of those countries that intend, at all cost, to maintain their monopoly on the world's material wealth. These events are yesterday's history: daily provocations of the three countries, so direct and preordained in form that there are few precedents in history. The only possible outcome of these provocations and acts of hostility was the extension of the war to the whole world.

The plot that has long been brewing against the Tripartite Nations is now an open, unscrupulous free-for-all. Today our enemies show no restraint—not even in public speech, where they are usually more cautious—in proclaiming that the ultimate goal of their war is the complete and definitive destruction of the three peoples.

Of course, among our common enemies, there may be voices that are more clear or more ambiguous in this regard, but the desire is always the same: to erase from the history of the years to come the names of Italy, Germany, and Japan.

This is the reality that should be held fast before us, in this, the roughest period of our struggle. We must not delude ourselves, or let ourselves be deceived. Italy is on its knees, but not down for the count. From the most bitter of experience, Italy knows the minds of our enemies, the reality that lurks under the lure of propaganda.

To save ourselves and to save the future of our sons, the path of history and the road of destiny must be followed to the end, regardless of the obstacles, the sacrifices, and sufferings. Only thus can a people provide proof of its maturity, and its right to create its own future.

I ask Italians to look at the sublime proofs of patriotism and valor provided by the people of Germany and Japan, and to restore within their spirits, shaken by sudden betrayal, the power of faith. I ask Italians to reflect upon the armistice conditions, which were also imposed upon other countries after Italy, and which recall the historic words: "woe to the vanquished."[32]

The Italian Social Republic represents the Italy that keeps its word, and considers honor the highest virtue among men, as a safeguard of both the present and the future.

Germany, Japan, and Italy cannot be conquered by the weight of gold nor by their enemies' vast hatred, nor by their material resources.

Fascist Republican Italy faithfully reaffirms the Pact that binds it to its loyal allies, confident in the justice of resisting and fighting until victory.

---

[32] [TN.] "*Guai ai vinti*": *Vae victis.*

Speech to the Blackshirts of the "Aldo Resega" Black Brigade, October 14th, 1944

What a joy it is to see once more the faces of comrades I knew in the early days, when, as today, we faced a world that was overthrown through tough battles and cruel sacrifices.

Even back then, everyone, from the reddest to the blackest, was against us, and our cause seemed doomed. If the cause triumphed, it was because it carried within itself the reasons for its rise and affirmation.

Once again, I see comrades who despite the passing of years and the many betrayals of the unfortunate summer, have remained faithful to the flag, and intend to remain so, no matter the circumstances.

Your Black Brigade bears the irreproachable name of Resega, a valiant fighter, a generous heart, an exemplary citizen who consecrated his faith with blood. It may be said that he came from the people and he died for the people, because the assassins who were paid by the enemy to eliminate him came from outside the people's community.[33]

---

[33] [TN.] *Comunità popolare*, the Italian translation of the German *Volksgemeinschaft*, an important concept connoting a form of racial unity.

All of you, from the leader to the lowest-ranking soldier, are strictly bound to conduct yourselves impeccably, according to the formal law and custom of Fascism, because nothing must sully the name and memory of that soldier of the Nation and Fascism.

From the reports that have reached me, I conclude that your Brigade is composed of robust, courageous comrades, for whom combat is second nature, and love of Italy a fundamental fact of the soul.

The military structure given to the party last June is in perfect harmony with the duties of the party itself in the current period of national history, which is dominated by war, and the black, unspeakable, shameful betrayal of September 8th.

What peace has unconditional surrender brought to the people? War was declared on October 13th against yesterday's allies, and the current plan is to declare war on Japan. To the war already underway in Italy will be added another, in the distant expanse of the Pacific, where Italian sailors are supposed to die for the Anglo-Saxon plutocracies, and pay the debt of gratitude toward America, for its recent, much flaunted "aid" of a purely electoral nature, a drop of water in the arid desert of Italian misery and despair.

At the Verona assembly, the Republican Fascist Party laid out its postulates. If the events of the war have delayed the application of some, this does not mean they have changed. In moments of high moral and political tension the watchwords must be few and extremely clear.

To whoever might still ask: "What do you want?" we respond with three words which sum up our program. They are: "Italy," "Republic," "Socialization."

For we enemies of generic, concordatory patriotism, which is at base only an alibi, tending toward compromise and defection, *Italy* means *honor*; and honor means keeping one's word, essential for the good reputation of individuals as well as peoples; and keeping one's word means collaborating with allies, in work and in combat. Everyone should recall—following the examples of history—that traitors, in politics and war, are used but despised.

It is in this very moment, with Germany engaged in a supreme battle, and eighty million Germans becoming eighty million soldiers, tightened into one effort of resistance that has something of the superhuman; it is precisely in this moment, with the enemy anticipating, in their hopes and illusions, a victory they will never achieve, because Germany will never capitulate, because capitulation for Germany would mean political, moral, and physical death; it is in this moment that we reaffirm our total solidarity with National Socialist Germany, which is the Germany that fights with a courage and virtue that may be called "Roman," and that earns recognition and admiration even from the enemy, when they are not totally blinded and stultified by hatred.

Let this be clear to all. This is the unbending attitude of Republican Italy. The series of betrayals by which the House of Savoy—from Carlo Alberto to Vittorio Emanuele III—dishonored itself, resulted in the fall of the Monarchy. Our Italy is republican. North of the Apennines there exists the Italian Social Republic. And this *Republic* will be defended inch by inch, to the last province, the last village, the last farmhouse. Whatever may happen on our territory during this war, the idea of the *Republic*, founded on Fascism, has now entered the spirit and customs of the people.

The third term of our program, *socialization*, has to be considered as the consequence of the first two terms, Italy and Republic. *Socialization* is nothing more than our very own Italian, human, practical realization of socialism; and I say "our" insofar as it makes labor the unique subject of the economy, while rejecting the mechanical levelling that does not exist in nature, and is impossible in history.

All those whose minds are clear of prejudice and sectarianism can recognize themselves in that trinomial: *Italy, Republic, Socialization*. With these terms we intend to summon the best elements of our working people on the political stage.

The capitulation of September signals the dishonorable liquidation of the bourgeoisie, generally considered the ruling class. This was a scandalous spectacle, of barely believable abjection, of sordid displays of asocial and anti-national egotism.

Those who adapt their feelings and opinions according to the circumstances of the war are, as always, hardly deserving of compassion or—in some cases—contempt. For many, emotional ups and downs preclude any positive analysis. A complete and universal judgment cannot be based on momentary impressions, which are often provoked by the thunder of enemy propaganda.

Not only will Germany never capitulate—and given that its enemies intend to annihilate Germany as a state and as a race, it simply cannot capitulate—it also still has many arrows in its quiver, besides unanimity and the iron will of its people.

Our enemies are in a rush and even say as much. While our sorrows are many, is there anyone so wilfully naive as to believe that in England, Russia, or even the United States everything is proceeding in the best possible way? Is it really possible to claim that there is not a sufficiently large group of intelligent people in England who are asking themselves if going up against so-called German imperialism is worth the effort; to lose hundreds of thousands of men, as well as all their positions in the Far East; to provoke the emergence of a Slavic imperialism that has already grabbed hold of Europe, from the Vistula to the Baltic, and—a painful enough fact for London—the Mediterranean. Can we not already hear demands that the haughty and absurd Casablanca formula of "unconditional surrender" be reviewed, so that it does not lead to the further sacrifice of millions of human lives? The greatest massacre of all time has a name: *Democracy*. Under this word hides the voracity of Jewish capitalism, which seeks to realize, through the slaughter of men and the destruction of Christian Civilization, the scientific exploitation of the world.

Realizing these truths within your own spirit means acknowledging that at a certain moment events will take a different turn, and that future developments of the war, in which science will have supreme importance, will stop the premature victory chants in the throats of the enemy. In this phase of the war, we intend to eliminate the internal accomplices of the enemy, and enlist all Italians who accept our tripartite program.

Whatever happens, we will not deviate from a single line of the program that I wanted to present to you, my dear comrades of the Black Brigade, the expression and honor of the firstborn *fascio*.

In vain—under the protection of foreign, mercenary bayonets—the men of unconditional surrender, of disgrace and cowardice, doggedly persist in the persecution of Fascists and Fascism. All they accomplish is documenting its irrepressible continuation. Six whole political parties are artificially cemented by a bond that is purely negative: the purifying, iconoclastic persecution of Fascism. They only do this because they know that that which is presumed dead is still alive; that it is still in the air that they breathe, in the things they encounter at every step, in the indelible material and spiritual signs that it has left everywhere. No human force can erase from history that which has already entered history as a reality and faith.

Over the last twenty years, in the shadows of the black banners, in peace and in war, in Italy, in Europe, in Africa, tens of thousands of Fascists, the flower of the Italian race, have fallen. They constitute the imperishable testimony and safeguard of Fascism, and its heroic expression.

Go to your Milanese Comrades, and bring them my greetings, the echo of my certainty in a victorious conclusion for Italy and for Europe, in this colossal clash of civilization that takes its name from Fascism.

Speech to the Legionaries of the Guard on the Anniversary of the March on Rome, October 28th, 1944

Legionaries!

Today, October 28th, on the anniversary of an event full of destiny for Italy and the world, I have the honor of presenting you with the battle flag. I entrust it to you in the name and in the memory of our innumerable, glorious fallen, whose memory you will honor in the manner worthy of soldiers, by always and everywhere fulfilling your duty.

The flag of the Italian Social Republic is the symbol of our absolute faith in the reconquest of the country; it is the pledge of our no less absolute faith in our intrepid ally; it is certainty in our victorious future. The flag is the soul of our souls. Receiving it, you take a solemn oath that it will never—never! —be stained by dishonor and cowardice, and that it will always, in peace and in war, be defended and consecrated by blood.

Legionaries! Meditate on my words, and let them guide you in your lives as Italians and as Fascists.

Speech at the Lirico Theater in Milan, December 16th, 1944

Comrades, dear comrades of Milan!

I'll dispense with any preamble and get right to the heart of the matter.

Sixteen months after the unconditional surrender, imposed and accepted according to the democratic and criminal Casablanca formula, an evaluation of these events once more begs the question: who was the betrayer? And who has suffered, and suffers, the consequences of this betrayal?

Let us be clear: this is not about some judgement based on historical revision, nor, in any shape or form, a justification. Though such justification may have been attempted by some neutral paper, we reject it in the most categorical manner, based on both the substance, and, secondarily, the source from which it comes.

So who was the betrayer? The unconditional surrender announced on September 8th, 1943, was wrought by the Monarchy, by court circles, by the plutocratic currents of the Italian bourgeoisie, by certain clerical powers joined in this instance with Masonic forces, and by the General Staff, who no longer believed in victory and turned to Badoglio. As early as May, May 15th to be precise, the ex-King noted in his diary—which has recently entered our possession—that there was a need to "uncouple" from the alliance with Germany. Without a shadow of doubt, it was the ex-King who ordered the surrender, and it was Badoglio who carried it out.

But before September 8th, there had to be July 23rd, meaning the coup d'état and regime change. The justification for surrender, and thus the impossibility of pushing ahead with the war, would be refuted forty days later, with the declaration of war against Germany on October 13th. This declaration was not just symbolic, because—even if only in terms of logistics and labor—collaboration began between Badoglio's Italy and the "allies," and the fleet, built entirely by Fascism, was passed into enemy hands and began immediate operations with the fleets of the enemy. Through so-called co-belligerence, war was pursued, not peace, and the Nation's entire territory was converted into one big battlefield, meaning one big ruin. Instead of peace, they were planning the participation of Italian troops and ships in the war against Japan.

It follows that it is the Italian people, above all, who have suffered the consequences of this betrayal. It is clear that it is not the Italian people who have betrayed our German ally. Except for sporadic cases, the Army units disbanded without any resistance to the German orders to disarm. Many units stationed outside the mainland, as well as Air Force units, immediately rallied behind the German forces in the tens of thousands. To the last man, all the Militia formations—minus a battalion in Corsica—also joined the Germans.

The so-called P44 plan—which will be discussed during the upcoming trial of the generals, and which foresaw the immediate switching of sides, as the King and Badoglio had preordained—did not find any purchase among the commanders. This is proven by the trial taking place in Bonomi's Italy, against a group of generals who refused to obey the orders contained in the plan. These orders were also refused by commanders deployed beyond Italy's borders.

Nevertheless, if such commanders avoided the worst, namely the extreme disgrace of stabbing our three-year allies in the back, their conduct, from the national perspective, has been disastrous. Had they listened to their conscience and sense of honor, they would have taken their weapons and equipment to our ally. This would have preserved our territorial and political positions; our flag would not be absent from lands where so much Italian blood has been spilled; the organic integrity of the armed forces would have been maintained; the compulsory internment of hundreds of thousands of soldiers would have been avoided, along with their immense, and above all moral, suffering; our ally would never have been overburdened with new, unforeseen military demands, which had consequences for the whole war plan. These are specific responsibilities that affect the Italian people above all.

It must nevertheless be recognized that the betrayals of the summer of 1944 were even more disgraceful, with Romanians, Bulgarians, and Finns ignominiously capitulating and switching sides— the Bulgarians without even firing a single shot—in the space of twenty-four hours, and attacking German units with all their mobilized forces, making withdrawal an arduous and bloody process. Here, in its absolute repugnance, betrayal reached a state of perfection. In comparison, the Italian people committed only a minor degree of betrayal, while the degree to which they have suffered, I won't hesitate to say, is superhuman. And that is not all: while a section of the population did accept surrender, due to foolishness or exhaustion, others immediately rallied behind Germany.

It is time to say to Italians and their German and Japanese comrades that the contribution made by Republican Italy to the common cause, from September 1943 onward, despite the temporary reduction in territory, is by far superior to what is commonly believed.

For obvious reasons, I cannot go into great detail about the figures showing Italy's total economic and military contributions. On September 30th, our collaboration with the Reich in terms of soldiers and workers amounted to some 786,000 men.[34] This number is indisputable, since it comes from a German source. We also have to add the former military internees:[35] hundreds of thousands of men injected into German production, and tens of thousands more who were already in the Reich, as free workers in the factories and fields.

Considering the evidence, Italians in the Social Republic have the right, once and for all, to hold their heads high and demand that their efforts be valued by all members of the Tripartite Pact with an equal sense of comradeship.

Just yesterday we had Eden's declarations on the losses inflicted against Great Britain while defending Greece. For three years, Italy has inflicted the harshest blows against the English, and in its turn, sacrificed assets and blood. But this is still not enough.

In 1945, Italy's participation in the war will undergo major developments, with the gradual reinforcement of our military

---

[34] [TN.] Error in RC: "7,896."
[35] [TN.] "Military internees" (Militärinternierte) was a designation created by the Germans for Italian soldiers captured on German territory in the days that followed the armistice between Italy and the Allies on September 8th, 1943.

organizations entrusted to the loyalty and proven experience of that soldier who goes by the title of Marshal of Italy, Rodolfo Graziani. In the tumultuous period of transition, autumn and winter of 1943, more or less autonomous military formations arose around men who, from past experience and their charisma as leaders, knew how to rustle up their own combat units. Individuals, battalions, regiments, and specialists were enlisted. It was the old commanders who sent out the call: an excellent initiative, especially when it comes to morale. But modern war requires unity. It is toward unity that we march.

I dare believe that Italians of all persuasions will be happy the day when all the armed forces of the Republic are joined in one body, and there is a single police force, both working together according to their functions, both living deep within the climate and spirit of Fascism and the Republic. In a war like the one we currently face, which has assumed the character of a war of politics, "political" has become an empty, obsolete term.[36] "Politics" is the confident, fanatical adherence to the idea for which one goes to war, while political activity is what the soldier, loyal to his orders, has no time to explain, since his politics must be the preparation for combat, as well as the example he gives to his comrades in peace and war.

On September 15th, the National Fascist Party became the Republican Fascist Party. At the time, there was no shortage of diseased or mentally unsound elements who would ask if it would not be shrewder to eliminate the word "Fascism" and put exclusive emphasis on "Republic." I rejected this useless, spineless suggestion, just as I reject it today. It would have been both cowardly and

---

[36] [TN.] *Apoliticità* in RC, *politicità* in OO.

erroneous to lower our banner, which is consecrated by so much blood, and to turn the idea that is the watchword in this battle of continents into a kind of contraband. Had we engaged in such a ruse, we would never have been able to face ourselves again.

Still and always calling ourselves Fascists—and consecrating ourselves to the cause of Fascism, as we have done from 1919 to today, and as we shall do tomorrow—we have given direction to our action, especially in the political and social domains. In truth, instead of "direction," it is much more accurate to say: a return to the original positions.

It is a matter of historic record that up to 1922 Fascism had republican tendencies. There is no need to explain why the 1922 insurrection spared the Monarchy. From the social point of view, the program of Republican Fascism is nothing but the logical continuation of those splendid years that stretch from the Labour Charter to the conquest of the Empire. Nature does not move in leaps and bounds, not even in economics. It was necessary to lay the foundations with the trade union laws and corporate bodies before we could take any further steps toward socialization. As far back as the first meeting of the Council of Ministers, September 27th, 1943, I declared that the "Republic would be unitary in the political domain and decentralized in the administrative domain, and that its social content would be given particular emphasis, so that it could resolve at least the most pressing aspects of the social question, namely establishing the position, function, and responsibility of labor in a truly modern national society."

During that same meeting, I took the first step toward achieving the broadest possible national harmony, by announcing that the

Government would rule out repressive measures against anti-fascist elements.[37]

In October, I drafted and revised what Italian political history has come to call the "Verona Manifesto," which established in a few relatively clear points the program, not so much of the party, but of the Republic. These points were more precisely developed on November 14th, two months after the constitution of the Republican Fascist Party.[38] After saluting the fallen of the Fascist cause, and after reaffirming the absolute necessity of continuing to fight alongside the Tripartite Powers and reconstituting the Armed Forces, the eighteen programmatic points of the PFR National Assembly "Manifesto" were set down.[39]

Now it is time to look at what has been done, what has not been done, and, above all, why it has not been done.

The "Manifesto" began with a demand to convene the Constituent Assembly, and laid out its composition, such that "the Constituent Assembly be a synthesis of all the Nation's values." But the Constituent Assembly was never convened. This postulate was never realized, and we can even say that it will not be realized until the war is over. Frankly, given how military operations were going, I thought it redundant to convene the Constituent Assembly when the territory of the Republic could in no way be considered definitive. It seemed

---

[37] [TN.] See OO, 6: "There is no plan, except in verified cases of violence, to enact any general repressive measures against those who, in a moment of infantile temerity, believed that a military government would be the most apt to realize a regime of unlimited liberty. Nor is there any question of enacting specific measures against those who professed their more or less active anti-fascism on July 26th and during the days that followed."

[38] [TN.] *Costituzione* in RC, *ricostituzione* ("reconstitution") in OO.

[39] [TN.] *Partito Fascista Repubblicano*, the Republican Fascist Party.

premature to create a genuine state, subject to rule of law, with all the associated institutions, when there were no armed forces to uphold it. A state with no armed forces at its disposal is anything but a state.

It was said in the "Manifesto" that no citizen could be held for more than seven days without an order from the Judicial Authority. This law was never introduced. The reasons are to be found with our police forces and those of our allies, as well as the actions of outlaws who have caused such questions to slide into a context of civil war, based on reprisals and counter-reprisals. Certain incidents have aroused the speculation of anti-fascists, who distort the reality and make the usual generalizations.

I must make it as clear as possible that certain methods are deeply repugnant to me, even if they are deployed only sporadically. The state, as such, cannot adopt laws that debase it. For centuries we have spoken of the law of retaliation. But that is a law, not a more or less personal whim.

Mazzini, the unbending apostle of the republican idea, at the dawn of the Roman Republic in 1849, sent a commissioner to Ancona to teach the Jacobins that it was permitted to fight the papists but not to kill them extrajudicially, or remove, as one would say today, the silverware from their houses. Whoever acts in such a way, especially if by chance they are a card-carrying party member, deserves a double sentence. In such cases, no severity is excessive if we want the party—as we read in the "Verona Manifesto"—to be a genuine "order of fighters and believers, a body of absolute political purity, worthy of being the custodian of the revolutionary idea." The personification of this type of Fascist was comrade Resega, whom I remember, and we all remember, with deep emotion, on the first anniversary of his death at the hands of the enemy.

With the formation of the Black Brigades, the party is becoming a genuine "order of fighters," and the Verona postulate has the character of a dogmatic, sacred duty. In article 5, where it is established that no party membership card should be required for a job or assignment, we have a solution to what I will call the problem of collaboration with other elements at the level of the Republic. In my telegram of March 10th, XXII to the provincial leaders,[40] this formula was revived and better explained. Thus, all talk about the problem of party plurality now seems obsolete.

Throughout history, among the forms in which the Republic as a political institution has manifested among various peoples, there have been many republics of the totalitarian kind, meaning those with a single party. I will not discuss the most totalitarian of these, namely that of the Soviets, but I will recall one that enjoys the sympathy of the high priests of the democratic gospel, the Turkish Republic, which is upheld by a single party, that of the people,[41] and a single youth organization, that of the "People's Houses."

At a given point in Italy's historical evolution, the presence of other groups, alongside the single party responsible for the overall direction of the state, can certainly bear fruit. As article 3 of the "Verona Manifesto" states, they have the right to scrutinize and responsibly criticize the actions of public authorities. Insofar as they are completely loyal to the "Italy, Republic, Socialization" trinomial, these groups are responsible for examining the measures of the government

---

[40] [TN.] XXII refers to the twenty-second year of the Fascist era.
[41] [TN.] The Republican People's Party.

and local authorities, and scrutinizing the methods by which those measures are implemented, as well as the public officeholders who are answerable to the citizen, as a soldier-worker contributing his labor.

The eighth point set down at the Verona Assembly established our foreign policy positions. It is often solemnly declared that the essential goal of the Republic's foreign policy is "the territorial unity, independence, and integrity of the Fatherland as demarcated by the seas and the mountains, by the sacrifice of blood, and by history." As for territorial unity, knowing Sicily and our Sicilian brothers, I refuse to take the so-called separatist movements seriously. They are contemptible mercenaries of the enemy. But this separatism could very well have a different motive: that our Sicilian brothers want to separate themselves from the Italy of Bonomi in order to join Republican Italy.

Leaving aside all our struggles, and once the "outlaw" phenomenon is liquidated, I am fully convinced that the moral unity among Italians will be infinitely stronger than it was before. It will be cemented by exceptional suffering, from which no family has been spared. And when, through moral unity, the soul of a people is saved, its territorial integrity and political independence are saved along with it.

At this point I should say a word about Europe as well as the concept of Europe. I will not linger on questions such as "what is Europe?" or "where does it begin and end, in geographic, historic, moral, and economic terms?" Nor will I ask whether a unification effort today would have more success than earlier efforts. Such questions would lead me too far astray. I will limit myself to saying that the creation of a European community is desirable and perhaps also possible. However, I must make it clear that we do not feel Italian because we are European; we feel European because we are Italian. This distinction is no mere nuance; it is fundamental.

Just as the nation is the result of millions of families with their own distinct physiognomies, though they may possess a national common denominator, each nation should join the European community as a well-defined entity, to ensure that the community itself does not capsize into socialist-style internationalism, or stagnate into some generic or ambiguous cosmopolitanism of the Jewish or Masonic stripe.

While certain points in the Verona program have been bypassed by the succession of military realities, more concrete achievements have been made in the social and economic domains.

Here the innovation has been quite radical. Points 11, 12, and 13 are fundamental. Detailed in the "premise for the new economic structure of the nation," these points have found their practical application in the socialization law. The interest that this has aroused around the world is truly great, and today, everywhere you look, even in the Italy dominated and tortured by the Anglo-Americans, every political program contains the socialization postulate. Workers, initially somewhat sceptical, have eventually understood its importance. Its realization is on course. The rhythm of this process would have been faster in different times, but the seeds have been sown. Whatever happens, these seeds are destined to germinate: to inaugurate that which eight years ago—here in Milan, in front of 500,000 cheering people—I prophesied as the "age of labor," in which the laborer would finally emerge from his economic and moral condition of wage earner to assume that of producer, with a direct interest in the development of the economy and the well-being of the Nation.

Fascist socialization is the logical and rational solution that avoids, on the one hand, the bureaucratization of the economy through state totalitarianism, and overcomes, on the other, the individualism of the liberal economy, which was an effective means of progress in the early stages of the capitalist economy, but is now out of sync with the new "social" demands within the communities of nations. Through socialization, the best elements drawn from the ranks of the laborers will be able to prove themselves. I am committed to proceeding in this direction.

I have entrusted two sectors to workers: local administration and food distribution. These sectors, crucial in the given circumstances, are now completely in the hands of the workers. They must—and I hope they will—put their specialized training and civic conscience to work. As you can see, things have been accomplished in the last twelve months, in the midst of incredible and growing difficulties, due to the objective conditions of the war and the blind opposition of those elements that sold out to the enemy, and the moral apathy that events have provoked in many segments of the population.

More recently, the situation has improved. The fence-sitters, those who were expecting the Anglo-Americans to arrive, are in decline. What is happening in Bonomi's Italy has disillusioned them. All that the Anglo-Americans promised has turned out to be a wretched, propagandistic ruse.

I believe I am right when I say that the population of the Po Valley not only do not want, but also scorn, the arrival of the Anglo-Saxons. They want nothing to do with a government that would return the reactionary, plutocratic, and dynastic forces to the North, even with

Togliatti as Deputy Prime Minister.[42] And these forces now openly enjoy the protection of England.

How ridiculous those republicans are who reject the Republic because it is proclaimed by Mussolini, only to succumb to the monarchy pushed by Churchill! Irrefutable proof that the Savoy Monarchy serves the interests of Great Britain, not of Italy!

There is no doubt that the fall of Rome is a climactic date in the history of the war. General Alexander himself, on the eve of the landing in France, declared that it was necessary to have a victory tied to a great name—and there is no greater or more universal name than that of Rome—for there to be an encouraging atmosphere. So the Anglo-Americans entered Rome on June 5th. The following day, the first Allied units landed on the coast of Normandy, between the Vire and Orne rivers. The months that followed were grueling, on all fronts where the soldiers of the Reich were and are deployed.

Germany called on all its reserves of manpower, with total mobilization entrusted to Goebbels, and with the creation of the *Volkssturm*.[43] Only a people such as the Germans, united around the Führer, could handle such enormous pressure. Only an army like that of the National Socialists could so rapidly overcome the crisis of July 20th and continue, according to the testimony of the enemy themselves, to fight on all fronts with exceptional tenacity and courage.

---

[42] [TN.] Palmiro Togliatti (1893–1964), leader of the Italian Communist Party (1927–1934 and 1938–1964) and Deputy Prime Minister of Italy from 1944 to 1945.
[43] [TN.] The *Volkssturm* was a national militia established on the orders of Hitler in September 1944.

There was a period in which the conquest of Paris and Brussels, the unconditional surrender of Romania, Finland, and Bulgaria, gave rise to a movement so euphoric that, according to the newspaper correspondents, it was thought that the war would be practically finished by Christmas, with the triumphant arrival of the Allies in Berlin.

In that period of euphoria, the Germans' new weaponry, improperly called "secret," was underestimated and scorned. Many believed that thanks to the use of such weapons, at a certain point—by the press of a button—the war would be finished in one go: this miraculous thinking is more imaginative than malicious. These are not *secret* weapons, but *new* weapons that, needless to say, are only secret insofar as they have not yet been deployed. That such arms exist, the English know from bitter reconnaissance. I am in a position to confirm that the first of these weapons shall be followed by others. That they are sufficient to quickly reestablish equilibrium and then hand the initiative to Germany, is, as far as we can humanly predict, almost certain, and will not require much time. After five years of war, nothing is more understandable than impatience, but this is about ordnance for which science, technology, and expertise must proceed with caution.

It is certainly true that the chain of surprises is not finished, and that thousands of German scientists are working day and night to increase the military potential of Germany. In the meantime, the German resistance becomes ever stronger, and many of the illusions cultivated by enemy propaganda have fallen. There are no cracks in the morale of the German people, who fully understand that their physical existence and future as a race are at stake. There is no sign of revolt, or even agitation, among the millions and millions of foreign workers, despite the insistent calls and proclamations of American generals. And an eloquent indicator of the spirit of the Nation is when the percentage of volunteers for the latest draft can almost form an entire class by itself.

Germany is up to the task of resisting and bringing the enemy plans to nought. Minimizing the loss of territories, conquered and preserved with blood, is not an intelligent strategy. The aim of war is not conquest or the conservation of territories, but rather the destruction of enemy forces, their surrender and the cessation of hostilities.

The German Armed Forces have not only not been destroyed; they are in fact in a stage of accelerating development and power. If we examine the situation from a political perspective, toward the end of 1944, fascinating events and dispositions have come to fruition.

Without exaggeration, it may be observed that the political situation today is not favorable to the Allies. First of all, in America, as in England, there are currents opposed to unconditional surrender. The Casablanca formula signifies the death of millions of young people: peoples such as the Germans and the Japanese will never hand themselves over to the enemy, whose unconcealed plan is the total annihilation of the Tripartite Countries.

This is why Churchill had to subject his hotheaded countrymen to a cold shower, and extend the completion of the war to summer 1945 for Europe, and 1947 for Japan.

The Soviet ambassador in Rome, Potemkin, once said to me: "The First World War bolshevized Russia; the Second will bolshevize Europe." This prophecy will never come to pass, but if it did, the main responsibility would lie with Great Britain. Politically, Albion is already defeated. The Russian forces are on the Vistula and the Danube—

halfway into Europe. The communist parties, the parties that act in the pay and on the orders of Stalin, already hold partial power in the West.

What does this "liberation" that the papers keep talking about mean for Belgium, Italy, and Greece? Misery, desperation, civil war. The "liberated" in Greece fire on the English "liberators," while the Russian communists fire on the British conservatives. In the face of this panorama, the English policy is to run for cover. Firstly, by liquidating in severe and bloody fashion, as in Athens, the partisan movements, which are the militant vanguard of the extreme left, namely bolshevism; and secondly, by supporting the democratic forces, which may be forceful, but shy away from the totalitarianism that finds its supreme expression in Soviet Russia.

Churchill categorically raised the anti-communist banner in his last speech to the House of Commons, and this cannot have pleased Stalin. Great Britain aims to reserve Western Europe as a zone of influence for democracy, which must not, under any circumstances, be contaminated by communism. But Churchill's "fronde" can only reach a certain point without the great Marshal of the Kremlin taking umbrage. Churchill wanted this zone of influence to be subsidized by an effectively anti-Russian pact between France, England, Belgium, Holland, and Norway.

The agreements between Stalin and De Gaulle buried this idea in its infancy. The idea had been advanced, on the instructions of London, by the Belgian Spaak. Now that the gambit has failed, Churchill has to, as the English say, eat his hat. He thinks of Russia entering the Mediterranean, and Russian pressure in Iran, and has to ask himself whether the Casablanca policy is not in fact—for "poor old England"—bankrupt. Squeezed by two military colossi of the East and

West—by insolent and insatiable cousins across the ocean, and by the inexorable Eurasians—Great Britain sees that its own imperial future, and thus its destiny, is at stake and in danger. The fact that political relations between the Allies have not improved, is proved by the grueling preparations for the new three-party conference.

Let us now speak of Japan, so far and yet so close. More than certain, it is a dogmatic truth that the Empire of the Rising Sun will never bend, and will fight until victory. In recent months the Japanese forces have been crowned with major successes. The enemy's much-vaunted landing in Leyte Island, one of the many hundreds of islands that form the Philippine Archipelago—a landing with primarily electoral goals—has, after two months, made almost no progress.

The will and soul of Japan is demonstrated by all those who have volunteered their death.[44] Not mere dozens, but tens of thousands of young men have as their motto: "one plane, one ship." And they prove it. Witnessing such superhumanly heroic determination, one can understand the attitude in certain American circles, where it is asked if it would not have been better—for Americans—if Roosevelt had kept his promise to American mothers that no soldier would be sent to fight and die abroad. As is customary in all democracies, he lied.

And for us, Italians of the Republic, it is cause for pride to have on our side, as faithful comrades, the soldiers, sailors, and airmen of the Tenno, whose deeds demand the admiration of the world.

Now I ask you: has the good seed of Italians, of healthy Italians—the best, who consider dying for the Fatherland eternal life—been spent? In the previous war, was there not an airman who, after failing to shoot

---

[44] [TN.] *Volontari della morte*, "volunteers of death."

down an enemy plane, flew directly into it, and fell with it? Have you forgotten his name? He was a humble sergeant: Dall'Oro.

In 1935, when England was trying to suffocate us in our sea, I took up the gauntlet and maneuvered 400,000 legionaries under the nose of Her Majesty's Navy, which was anchored in the ports of the Mediterranean, as the death squadrons were being formed in Rome. I must tell you, in truth, that the first on the list was the commander of the Air Force. Well, if it were necessary to form these squadrons again tomorrow, if it were necessary to show that the blood of the Roman legionaries still flows through our veins, would my appeal be met with silence?

We will defend, tooth and nail, the Po Valley; we want the Po Valley to remain Republican, before the time comes for all of Italy to be Republican. The day in which the Po Valley is polluted by the enemy, the destiny of the entire Nation will be compromised; but I sense and see that tomorrow an armed and unbending formation will rise up and make life practically impossible for the invaders. The entire Po Valley shall be Athens.

From what I have said to you, it is clear that not only has the enemy coalition not won, but that they will never win. The monstrous alliance of plutocracy and bolshevism may have been able to perpetrate its barbaric war like the commission of some terrible crime, which has brought down masses of innocent people and destroyed that which European Civilization took over twenty centuries to create. But it will not succeed in annihilating, with its darkness, the eternal spirit that built such monuments. Our absolute faith in victory does not rest on subjective or sentimental motives, but on positive and determined elements. If we were to doubt our victory, we would have to doubt the existence of He who rules, according to justice, the fates of men.

When we, as soldiers of the Republic, reestablish contact with the Italians on the other side of the Apennines, we shall have the gratifying surprise of finding more Fascism there than when we left it. The disillusion, the misery, the political and moral abjection explode not only from the old expression "it was better in the old days," but also from the creeping rebellion from Palermo to Catania, from Otranto to Rome itself, from every corner of "liberated" Italy.

South of the Apennines, the spirits of the Italian people burn with nostalgia. Enemy oppression on the one hand, and the government's beastly persecution on the other, only fuel the Fascist movement. Erasing all the external symbols was easy; suppressing the idea is impossible.

The six anti-fascist parties are scrambling to proclaim the death of Fascism, because they sense that it's still alive. Millions of Italians are comparing today with yesterday: when the flag of the Fatherland was flying from the Alps to Equatorial Somalia, and Italians were among the most respected peoples on earth.

There is no Italian whose heart does not race at the sound of an African name, the sound of a hymn that accompanied the Legions from the Mediterranean to the Red Sea, or the sight of a colonial helmet. From 1929 to 1939,[45] there have been millions of Italians who have experienced what may be defined as the epic of the Fatherland. These Italians are still there, suffering but still believing, and they are ready to close ranks and march for the reconquest of all that has been lost,

---

[45] [TN.] "From 1939" in RC, "from 1929 to 1939" in OO. (OO, 138)

and is presided over today, from the Libyan dunes to the Ethiopian Ambas, by thousands upon thousands of our fallen, the flowers of innumerable Italian families who have not forgotten, and cannot forget. Already the signs of revival can be seen, here above all, in pioneering, commanding Milan, which the enemy has savagely struck, but has never caused to bend.

Comrades, dear Milanese comrades!

It is Milan that must give—that will give—the men, the arms, the will, and the signal of reconquest!

December 16th, 1944—After the Speech at the Lirico Theater— Il Duce Speaks Again in the Piazza San Sepolcro, Addressing the "Comrades of the Firstborn Fascio"

Comrades!

Now that there's no screen of papers before me, I feel like I am in more direct communication with your spirit. I speak to you; we look each other in the eyes; we feel our souls vibrate in unison, burning with the one flame: profound love for this Italy that was once great and that, no matter the sacrifice, must be great once more.

Comrades!

One does not return after so many years to your and our city; one does not return to this place without being gripped by deep and overpowering emotion. This very square is tied to an event of not only Italian history, but world history.

Today, during the brief trip through your city, I was left with a clear impression of the terrible wounds that a barbarous and abject enemy has inflicted. The Milanese people have proudly withstood these blows and demonstrated their robust moral foundation and strength.

Milan has shown once again that it knows how to welcome, within its hospitable walls, refugees from every region of Italy. It has demonstrated that the Ambrosian soul considers all Italians brothers, from the Alps to the farthest islands.

Step by step, as the enemy advances toward the North, they meet hard, hostile faces and sniper fire. Florence gave an example to fill every Italian with pride. This example has been imitated by Forlì. And I am certain that tomorrow it will be the same in every city, because now everyone knows what these "liberators" are all about. They bring nothing but political slavery, economic servitude, and moral abjection.

A people worthy of this name is never defeated, until they lay down their arms. And we will not lay down our arms until the day of victory.

Milan, December 16th, 1944. Mussolini, beside Alessandro Pavolini, speaks to soldiers and citizens from the roof of an armored car. This would be the last large crowd he would greet, on a day crowned by his famous speech at the Lirico Theater.

Speech to the Muti Legion, December 17th, 1944[46]

If any of our multicolored enemies—and I say multicolored because besides a few white bastards they are people of all the races—had witnessed today's procession along via Dante, they would have been convinced that, despite the gray autumn, the great spring of the Fatherland is upon us. I feel it in your enthusiasm; I read it in your eyes.

I know that the echo of the Milanese demonstrations has already reached the legionaries of the four divisions that have trained in Germany under severe discipline, and are ready to liberate the soil of the Fatherland. Each and every one of you must feel like a soldier, and make this order his own: one and all for Italy.

---

[46] [TN.] December 16th in RC.

Speech to the Legionaries of the Republican Guard, December 18th, 1944[47]

Legionaries of the Guard!

I have granted you the supreme honor of forming the first combat arm within the Republican Army. You must, at every instant and in the fulfillment of your duty—in peace and in war—be worthy of this privilege.

I am certain that this will be the case, because I know that the faith that animates you is still that of the glorious *squadrismo* that constructed the Blackshirt Revolution.

I will summarize your orders in one word: you must be irreproachable, such that the Italian people will be proud of you at every moment.

---

[47] [TN.] December 16th in RC.

Sailors of the Decima Flottiglia MAS

Speech to the Female Auxiliary Service of the Armed Forces, December 18th,1944[48]

Comrade auxiliaries!

You have the privilege of taking the oath on a memorable anniversary in the history of the Fatherland. Nine years ago, fifty-two states, maneuvered as always by London, sided with the iniquitous Genevan Sanhedrin against Fascist Italy, by trying to compromise its future by the most wretched means: starvation.

The Italian people, amassing around the sign of the Littorio, accepted the Genevan challenge, and on December 18th, 1935 responded in the most Roman of ways. Millions of women gathered around the sacred altar of the Fallen,[49] and offered their gold, including their wedding rings.

This became known as—and will always be known as—"the day of faith," a spontaneous gesture by Italian women, who authentically emulated the women of Ancient Rome.

---

[48] [TN.] December 16th in RC.
[49] [TN.] The Altar of the Fatherland, which is also the site of the Tomb of the Unknown Soldier.

The Italian people resisted, fought, won, and in the end got the better of the enemy coalition.

I am certain that no matter the circumstances, and with the purest souls, you will stay true to the oath you have taken today. Remember: you do not take the oath for me, but for Italy.

Volunteers of the Female Auxiliary Service

Speech at the Tomb of Gabriele D'Annunzio in Gardone, March 1st, 1945

For the last seven years, absent and present, he who, for fifty years, with poetry and action, on the battlefields of earth, sea and sky, exalted like no other the virtues of our race, has dwelled here.

Those who were familiar with him know that he never liked to be called a Poet-Soldier. But this is what he was, in the purest sense of the term, in its supreme incarnation, from Tyrtaeus to Mameli.[50]

Today he is here among his intrepid legionaries, who find their definitive repose in the marble tombs that will defy time and generations. He is here among us, and yet never, in this time of universal palingenesis, have we so acutely felt the absence of his voice.

With what words, with what scorch marks of infamy, would he have branded the deeds of the fugitive and traitor king, and his no less wretched accomplices in unconditional surrender? And how, during another wretched moment in our Fatherland's history, could he have failed to find the words that would drive the battered and isolated

---

[50] [TN.] Goffredo Mameli (1827–1849), Italian poet who wrote the lyrics for *Il Canto degli Italiani*, the Italian national anthem. Wounded while fighting the French during the siege of Rome, he died of sepsis several days later.

people to battle and honor, alongside our German comrades, who with inexhaustible courage stand up to the whole world?

And how could he not have openly signed his support for our Republic, he who in 1920—with he who speaks to you now—traced the outlines of a march on Rome?

Unexpected death, the kind that all fighters favor, caught him at his desk when he was still full of vigor. The passing of time had never touched him, at his desk for Italy and always for Italy.

The petty betrayers of Rome, who never appreciated his multifaceted greatness, tried to subject him to a posthumous moral trial, yet only provided incontrovertible proof of their own abjection.

For some time after his death, there was a certain silence around his name: the dead demand some solitude. Today, the rhythm of his poetry presses upon our spirits. It is, for us, the standard-bearer of the reconquest of our nation.

And now that I have spoken to you, I almost have the impression that the spirit of the Poet, blowing among these olive trees and cypresses, is asking me: "Why have you commemorated me? Am I really so dead that I have to be commemorated?"

It is indeed difficult to commemorate a man with a manifold soul like that of Gabriele D'Annunzio.

Our response to him is: no, Commander.

You are not dead, and you will never die as long as there is a peninsula called Italia planted in the middle of the Mediterranean. You are not dead, and you will never die as long as there is a city in the center of that peninsula to which we will return and which is called Roma.

March 23rd, 1945. Mussolini reviews the National Republican Guard at the Salò headquarters, on the twenty-sixth anniversary of the first Fasci di combattimento.

Speech to the Officers of the National Republican Guard, March 6th, 1945

This, comrade officers of the Guard, may be the first in a series of encounters through which I intend to reestablish moral as well as physical contact with you and your legionaries.

Before relating some things that should interest you, I want—not as a mere formality, but from a deep spiritual impulse, and confidence in interpreting your feelings—to address my heartfelt salutations to the 2,763 legionaries who have fallen since September 1943, for remaining loyal to the fascist idea, for remaining loyal, above all, to the destiny of the Fatherland. I would also like to recall the 3,707 wounded. And I salute, not as an empty formality, our comrades who have spent months or even years in the Balkans.

They are justified in feeling forgotten. Many have not seen Italy for forty months. During this period, they have only very rarely received word from their families, never had a day of leave, and have suffered— much more than those who remain in Italy—all the consequences of September's betrayal. They have seen with their own eyes the scorn of the populations we used to administer; they have experienced the deep humiliation of the flag being lowered in territories that had been bathed in the blood of Italian soldiers, while Italian civilians were abandoned to reprisals.[51]

I believe that their suffering has been enough to leave an indelible furrow in their souls. Now and then they write to me, and their morale is still very high. They have fought alongside our German comrades in circumstances that are always extraordinarily difficult. They have left hundreds of fallen comrades in those treacherous Balkan regions, which will always be a land of murky races.[52]

Comrade officers!

Your contact with the legionaries must be constant. The era of the officer keeping his distance from his men is over. You must remain with your legionaries, live with your legionaries, observe them, interpret them even when they do not know how to express themselves. You must be curators of souls, not just men who give orders. Obedience must always be prompt, blind, and absolute, but today it must also be intelligent. He who obeys must be convinced that his duty is to obey. In this way, your men will be at the ready, and you can ask of them that which must be done. But above all, you must lead by example.

The soldier is reflected in his officer, and the legionary should find in his officer his guide, his teacher, a man who is animated by an indomitable faith. You must be the propagators of this absolute and dogmatic faith in victory. He who doubts is already a loser, preparing to kneel before the winner. You are only defeated the day you declare

---

[51] [TN.] In OO, "reprisals by primitive people." (OO, 162)

[52] [TN.] *Di torbida razza. Torbido* typically refers to muddy water, or shady situations or behavior. It has a more moral connotation than the English "turbid."

yourself defeated. From that day on, there is a loser and a winner, and never before that.

Secondly: collaboration with our German comrades should be daily, sincere, loyal, and without reserve. Language difficulties and differences in temperament may occasionally make themselves felt, but we must remember that we are in the same boat, and that we want to reach the same port, victoriously, together.

Thirdly: with the utmost sincerity, I can say that I do not like those who are always counting what they or others receive. This is not the behavior of a legionary, but that of a mercenary. By this I do not mean that life's necessities should be left unsatisfied, or that we should not think of our families—of your families—but comparisons are always odious and often irrelevant, because any inequalities will be remedied.

Esprit de corps is a wonderful thing.

Each soldier should be proud to be fighting under his respective unit. But when this spirit is concerned with the group alone, it becomes grotesque and worthy of ridicule. On the contrary, there must be consciousness of a duty that is fulfilled with a purity of spirit, an ever-deeper tradition, which becomes the spiritual heritage of the group to which the soldier belongs.

There is no doubt that the July 25th coup d'état was a work of perfection, a masterpiece. Everything—personnel, location, timing—was prepared to the last detail. If the Royal Chief of Staff had prepared his battles with such precision, I would be speaking to you from a square in Cairo, instead of a suburb in Brescia. Fascism was obviously taken by surprise. So let's make one thing clear: the betrayed may sometimes be simpleminded, but the betrayer is always a scoundrel.

Many leaders engaged in the betrayal, but the bulk of fascists was taken by surprise. For a long time, the perpetrators had one dilemma: what would the Militia do?

If the Militia had stood guard in the interior, it would have been said that they were shirking, that they weren't fighting the war. And it is true that between remaining in the interior and going to the front, all legionaries prefer the second option by a long shot. But the traitors, meanwhile, achieved their goal of having them out of the way. The best of the Militia were abroad, beyond the borders of the mainland, and Fascism was faced with the near-impossibility of mounting immediate resistance.

There was a phase of uncertainty. People were confused: "the war goes on."

The other traitor, the Savoyard, who was continuing a long tradition that began with Carlo Alberto, declared that there was no need for recriminations. The provincial leaders of Fascism were recalled. The confusion was great. Evidently, we were dealing with the immaturity of at least one segment of the Italian people. One cannot pretend that twenty years of the regime is enough to enact a profound transformation on the moral structure of a people. That would require several generations. From 1530 on—from the fall of the Florentine Republic—there were two centuries free of warmongering,[53] during which, excluding Piedmont, no part of Italy had armed forces. There was a grand duke of Tuscany who even had a formula to justify, to some extent, this lack of bellicosity: "Big princes: barracks and cannons; little princes: villas and lodges."

---

[53] [TN.] Three in RC, two in OO.

The treaty of Westphalia shattered Germany into 303 states: a real headache, a crossword puzzle. And when Napoleon established the first draft, he found himself with a mass of men from which he thought he'd never be capable of sculpting a mass of soldiers worthy of the name. And yet, Napoleon himself, in the memoirs written at Saint Helena, after seeing the Italian soldiers fight by his side in Russia—and here we must remember that the only units that did not abandon Napoleon during the retreat from Russia were Neapolitan cavalry squads and Tuscan scout units (while the French deserted him) —after seeing the Piedmontese fight at Austerlitz, he wrote that it was still possible, in the right circumstances, to draw valiant soldiers from the old Italian race, because when it came to personal courage, the Italian people, taken individually, had nothing to envy in any other people on earth.

The Italians who have no fear of laying their hides on the line are numerous: more than is thought.

As I was saying, we were taken by surprise. I will add that we will not be taken by surprise again. We have promised, as I declared in my speech in Milan, that we will defend the Po Valley, city by city, house by house. Preparing the legionaries for this defence is a sacred commitment that we must and will undertake. I am sure that every one of you will be proud to lead the legionaries to combat.

The Guard has already formed a division with anti-aircraft and anti-tank artillery. These lads may have shown some hesitation at first, but today they are delighted to take position by the cannon, the gaping mouth that speaks with a voice intelligible to all. By the end of the period of Fascism that accepted the monarchy, we were taken by surprise; we cannot and will not be taken by surprise in the phase of Fascism that is republican.

If later events allow us to break through the Apennines (no one can exclude the possibility), I believe we will be met by a wave of enthusiasm even greater than expected.

I have not said, this evening, anything exceptionally interesting. The important thing, comrade officers, is that you stand firm. I will finish where I began: get it into your heads that Germany cannot be beaten, for one very simple reason: for the Germans, as for the rest of us, this is a matter of life and death. All the cards are on the table. No one says to Germany, as they did in the era of Wilson's famous Fourteen Points: if you change the regime then things will be easier for you (which was never the case). Today, after Yalta, it is openly declared that Germany must be destroyed as a people.

It is clear that the German people, from the highest of citizens, the Führer, to the last of the workers, are engaged in a life and death struggle. For the German General Staff and the German people, all arms are now justified against succumbing.

What I have told you will be a guide and viaticum for what is your daily mission. It is—precisely—in difficult and extraordinary times that the mettle of souls is tested. Anyone can navigate peacetime.

You must meditate on my words and take them to your legionaries: turn what I have said into an instrument for your daily orientation and, above all, be convinced that Fascism cannot be erased from the history of Italy. Whatever they may do in occupied Italy, they will once again demonstrate their lack of intelligence. But whatever enters history can never be erased. The traces we have left in the products and spirits of Italians are too deep to imagine that these men, dug up from their graves—in which they lived until yesterday, and into which we should have definitively driven them—could fight and win against our generations and our ideas, which represent the life and the future of the Fatherland.

Mussolini reviews 5th Alpine Mobile Black Brigade Enrico Quagliata, active in Val Camonica.

Speech to the Officers of the National Republican Guard in the Milan Prefecture, the Afternoon of April 23rd, 1945[54]

Asvero Gravelli has brought you to me because you wanted to see me and hear my voice. You, many of you, will form the Arditi Officer Unit of the Guard. In just a moment you will have instructions for deployment. But first I must say that the events that are currently unfolding demand that you be ready and on your feet. You must fight like the heroic Fascists of Florence, Forlì, and Bologna, who contested the enemy at every step. This Fatherland of ours, worthy of adoration, must not perish; if Italy were to die, our lives would not be worth living! We will reach Valtellina to prepare for the last, desperate defense: to die with the sun on our face and our gaze turned to the mountain tops, the last smile of the Fatherland. The hour is grave, but whatever may be our destiny, veterans of the Militia, I yell the new and ancient battle cry: "One for all, all for one!"

---

[54] [TN.] Mussolini's final speech.

THE POLITICAL TESTAMENT
OF BENITO MUSSOLINI

Preface[55]

It is well known that, when he was arrested at Dongo, Mussolini had with him a large leather briefcase containing important documents. While these documents would certainly have been of great interest to recent history, so far history is ignorant of them. Perhaps they will have to be considered lost, because the briefcase disappeared and was never found.

Until this personal and confidential correspondence, which Mussolini was carrying and had to abandon—no one knows where, or how—after his arrest on the western shore of Lake Como, is rediscovered (if ever)—until that day, the words, writings, declarations, confessions, that he wrote, dictated, expounded, or pronounced during the last decade of his existence—and, in particular, between April 20th, 1945 and April 28th, at 4:00 p.m., when he and Clara Petacci, after having slept their last sleep at Germasino di Mezzegra, were shot dead—will be of acute interest and exceptional documentary value.

Mussolini had many things to say. The journals, the testimonies, the numerous interviews with resistance fighters, confirm what the former leader of the Social Republic, already sentenced to death,

---

[55] From Il testamento politico di Mussolini, Editore Tosi, Rome, 1948.

allegedly said himself at Mezzegra: "I want to speak one last time to the world, before I die. Nine times I was betrayed. The tenth time, I was betrayed by Hitler."

Of course, he was in no place to speak as he would have liked. What thoughts were driving him to ask for one last interview? Until today, we had no clue.

Not because the famous leather briefcase has finally been found; rather, because what we can justly call Mussolini's testament has been brought to light.

There can be no doubt about this. These last words were not only dictated by him. Two days after the typed manuscript had been drafted, Mussolini himself chose to review it, correct it, and initial the whole manuscript with his unmistakable M.

Now you ask: "Why would such an important document, such a vital testimony, only appear now?"

A more than natural question, and the answer could not be simpler: because the person who wrote down these declarations, the person to whom they were dictated, the fortuitous collector of Mussolini's ideas, of his will and desperate defence, had sworn to keep the contents of those pages a secret until three years after the death of Mussolini.

This, as we shall see, was the directly expressed will of Mussolini himself.

And this is why only now, three years after the tragedy of April 28th, 1945, the repository of Mussolini's last thoughts has suddenly appeared, freed from a vow of silence.

The document takes the form of an interview. The interviewer, Gian Gaetano Cabella, editor of the *Popolo di Alessandria*, was received in Mussolini's studio near the Milan Prefecture, on the afternoon of

April 20th, 1945. The document was then revised on April 22nd, seven days before Mussolini's death.

Needless to say, this is no ordinary interview. It consists of absolutely extraordinary declarations, expressed at a time when Mussolini was fully aware of the collapse and his own imminent demise.

When the trusted journalist returned on April 22nd, events had already precipitated, with a rhythm that allowed no more illusions. The Anglo-Americans were triumphantly approaching the Po. All hope for any form of resistance had vanished, whether from the German army or the fascists. The vast Alpine circle already echoed with the sinister "every man for himself." For this reason, Mussolini had a vision—perhaps still cloudy, but no less dramatic—of the approaching end. This would explain his last-minute orders for the loyal journalist: "If I should die, do not divulge what I have placed in your hands until three years after my death."

This is a document of exceptional historic and human importance. It is an extreme appeal to posterity, dictated by Benito Mussolini on April 20th, and corrected by him on April 22nd in a private room of the Milan Prefecture.

The Last Interview with Benito Mussolini, April 20th, 1945[56]

It was Minister Zerbino who communicated the invitation to me on April 19th. Mussolini would receive me the next day, in the Prefecture. I immediately had editions of the newspaper bound up: all the Milanese editions of September 1944 up to the latest edition of April 21st, 1945. I wanted to offer Il Duce the entire collection, together with brochures and circulation charts. The *Popolo*, beginning with eighteen thousand copies printed and sixteen thousand sold in its first year, was now selling 270,000 copies, not counting the special editions, which were also a major success. Demand was now exceeding circulation. Many comrades had given me writings and messages to present to Il Duce. I divided these papers into three categories:

---

[56] The man who writes is Gian Gaetano Cabella, the former editor of the *Popolo di Alessandria*, a paper that also published an edition in Milan in 1944, for the region of Lombardy. In April 1945, when Cabella heard of Mussolini's arrival in Milan via Villa Feltrinelli on Lake Garda, he immediately requested and obtained an audience with the leader of the Social Republic. We will leave the narration of the various phases of the interview to Cabella himself. It begins like any old conversation that Mussolini might have had with this or that newspaper editor. But very quickly, the interview assumes an exceptional scope: for this was to be the last interview granted by Mussolini, and one that Mussolini himself wanted to correct, review, and annotate before publication.

1) Those I would give him under any circumstances;

2) Those that were less important;

3) Those that I would give him only if the interview went particularly well.

I also prepared a brief report on the lengthy negotiations that I conducted with the partisans, who had invited me to contact some of their representatives. Without hesitation, I accepted the appointment, which took place on February 7th at Rondissone, near Turin. It was an interesting meeting, for many reasons, and allowed for a certain amount of understanding about the best interests of the country.

At 2:30 p.m. on, April 20th, I was in the Prefecture. In the first waiting area there were officers and senior officials walking around and talking. The prefect, head of the Private Secretariat, frequently crossed the hall between his office and Mussolini's study. In the other hall there was Colonel Colombo, commander of the Muti Legion, along with the deputy commander and others. At 3:00 p.m., I met with Commander Borghese accompanied by several officers and the Chief of Staff of the GNR (Black Republican Guard).[57]

The Minister Mezzasoma was speaking with a group of journalists, including Daquanno, Amicucci, and Gguglielmotti. Shortly after, Vittorio Mussolini also joined the group.

There was an apparent serenity among these people, and, especially in the first hall, a discrete silence. An officer of the German SS walked through, smoking. Guard duty was limited to the

---

[57] The GNR was in fact the *Guardia Nazionale Repubblicana*, founded December 8th, 1943, with domestic police and military functions.

Government Palace entrance, as well as two armed sentries (an SS soldier and a Guardia militiaman) at the back entrance that led from the court to the apartment occupied by Il Duce and members of the government.

At 3:20 p.m. the police commissioner arrived and spoke with Prefect Bassi. Shortly after, there emerged from Il Duce's study a man who must have been in there for twenty minutes. I forget who he was; perhaps Pellegrini. Then a doorman came, and closed the door behind him, but he was not fast enough to prevent me from seeing Mussolini seated behind a small desk. Meanwhile, my editor-in-chief arrived: Second Lieutenant of the Bersaglieri Galileo Lucarini Simonetti. Before working with me, he had been the editor of the *Leonessa*, a weekly of the Brescia Federation.

Finally, Il Duce's door opened. The doorman announced my name loudly. I hurried inside. I placed the bundles over a chair to my right, and saluted at attention. Mussolini greeted me with a smile. He rose to his feet and approached me. Suddenly I saw that Mussolini was in excellent health, contrary to the rumors. He was doing infinitely better than the last time I had seen him. It was December 1944, at his speech at the Lirico. The previous times he had received me— February, March, and August 1944—he never seemed so hearty. He had a tanned and healthy color, vivid eyes, brisk movements. He had also fattened up a little. In any case, the thinness that had struck me in February of the year before, which had given his face a hollow, emaciated look, was gone. Before this man who was now completely different, the memory of the other immediately vanished.

He was wearing a gray-green uniform with no decoration or rank. He placed his big glasses on the table, over a page full of notes in blue pencil. I noticed that the table was small: many files had been left on the other little table nearby. Others were simply lying on the floor, near the window. I would leave with the impression that on the desk there had been a crystal vase containing a red rose, but I cannot guarantee the accuracy of this detail. On a chair, I spotted three bags full of documents: two made of thick leather, the other of dark yellow hide.

Mussolini placed his right hand on my shoulder and asked me:

"What do you bring me that is good?"

His first words were a repetition of what he had said to me fourteen months earlier, though in an entirely different tone: slower, lower, more tired. I did not know how to respond at first. As usual, and as would often happen to others upon encountering this man, I felt somewhat disoriented. After a moment's hesitation, I responded that I was happy to see him again, and that I had brought him a collection of our newspapers. He slapped my shoulder, then stared at me and said:

"I praise you for all that you have done to consolidate the Social Republic. Pavolini mentioned your speech in Turin on March 23rd, and what a success it was. I never knew you were also an orator."

I offered him the collection of newspapers and showed him the graphs for circulation, sales, letters received. I handed him various writings by fascists, soldiers, youth. He lavished me with praise, especially for the three special editions, rich with illustrations, dedicated to "Stellassa" (Umberto di Savoia), "Pupullo" (Badoglio), and "Bazzetta" (Vittorio Emanuele III).

He leafed through the collection, pausing at certain editions. He laughed.

"The three illustrated editions for "Bazzetta," "Pupullo," and "Stellassa" are so well done. I really enjoyed them. What kind of circulation did they have?"

"270,000 copies were sold. There was a demand for 380,000, but there was a shortage of paper."

"You will have all the paper you need."

Still on his feet, he took his pencil and jotted a few notes in a notebook. Gaining confidence, I shared some unfortunate news about two Bolognese comrades. His face became sorrowful.

"I can get them 10,000 lira. Will that do?"

He wanted their names and addresses. He wrote them down in the notebook, and then asked me:

"Would you like anything from me?"

After a moment of confusion, I answered:

"I've already received my prize: the praise that you have given me. Is it too much to ask for a dedication?"

I showed him a large photograph. He stared at it for a moment, and shook his head. Clearly, he was not too pleased with the image. Then he returned to the table, sat down, took his pencil and wrote: "To Gian Gaetano Cabella, Pilot of the *Popolo di Alessandria*, with the soul of the old guard. B. Mussolini, April 20th, XXIII."[58]

After putting down the pencil, he wanted to see the charts. The circulation of the paper was shown in a diagram. There was an ascending line, with slight contractions here and there.

"To what do you attribute the drop in sales here?"
"I believe it is necessary every now and then, especially after editions that make a lot of noise, to publish some less colorful editions, without any hard-hitting headlines."

I then briefly explained the criteria that I followed and deemed correct, before adding:

"You have been my teacher. I still have my collections of <u>Avanti!</u> and <u>Popolo d'Italia</u>."

Mussolini shook his head, paused thoughtfully for a moment, and observed:

"There are born journalists just as there are born composers and engineers. Creating a newspaper is like experiencing the joy of maternity. Avoiding monotony is the right criteria. Trombones

---

[58] [TN.] XXIII refers to the twenty-third year of the Fascist era.

and bass drums alone do not make a concert. After their initial
shock, the public simply gets used to it. I see that you are also a
capable administrator. A real Genoan . . ."

He paused at the graph showing letters received from the public, and
remarked:

"Many anonymous readers, I see."
"About 10 percent of the letters we receive are anonymous.
However, when things are going well for the Axis, the proportion
of anonymous letters tends to shrink."

I told him that in Alessandria I had stuck the most amusing letters to
the wall.

Mussolini smiled:

"I've seen the photos of your offices."
"In March, of the 2,785 letters we received, 360 were anonymous."
**"More than 2,400 signed letters in a month is a lot. Do you
respond to all of them?"**

I told him that I respond personally to all of them, whether in the
"editor's replies" section, or, as in most cases, directly.

"I've noticed that you can reach a larger audience this way.
Anyone who receives a personal letter from the editor, especially
in a smaller city, will show it to other people. They automatically
become loyal propagandists."

Mussolini took the package of letters that I had brought along. I told him how I had divided them into three categories. I wanted him to have all of them.

"If I have the time, I will read them this evening."

Then he opened three letters that I had placed on top: one from a lady who lived near Turin; another from a young volunteer, Puni, from Turin; the third from a celebrity from Liguria.

"Thank the lady and the boy for me. Leave the other one for me: I'll respond directly. Is there anything else you would like to tell me?"

"I have two collaborators, a Fascist and an old Florentine socialist . . ."

Mussolini interrupted with the names of both, and added:

"Send them my regards. Tell them that I read the articles that they write with great interest."

I had the impression that the interview was drawing to a close. Mussolini reopened the collection of newspapers and eventually found the copies of Il *Monarchico,* which I had printed while in hiding and pretended it was an outlet of the C. Cavour monarchist group in Turin, as well as a copy of *Grido di Spartaco,* which I also published in hiding.

Mussolini laughed, and exclaimed:

"I love them. For this too I must commend you."

This gave me some encouragement:

"Duce, would you allow me to ask you some questions?"

Mussolini rose to his feet, and came up close to me. Looking me in the eye, he suddenly asked, with an accent and expression that I will never forget:

"Interview or testament?"

I was dumbfounded by the question, and did not know how to respond. My feelings did not escape Mussolini, who tried to dissolve my confusion with a warm smile.

"Sit here. Here is a pen and some paper. I am ready to answer your questions."

Greatly agitated, I sat to his left. His hand was close to mine. Many ideas were crowding into my mind, but they were all too vague. Finally, I formulated a generic enough question:

"What are your thoughts, what are your orders, in the present situation?"

Instead of "orders" I said "directions," but since it was left unchanged in the text that Mussolini reviewed, corrected, and signed the next day, I will leave it as he approved it. I must add that, while I took note with as much attention as possible of what Mussolini was saying to me, I could not, in the days that followed, relay the complete conversation with complete accuracy. Only now, with enough distance, can I remember with absolute precision. For this reason, I can now provide clarification where it was not possible at the time. This is why I am adding these notes, and the notes that follow.

To my question, Mussolini asked in turn:

"What would you do?"

I must have shown an involuntary sign of surprise. Mussolini touched my arm and smiled again:

"Don't be surprised. I ask everyone this. I want to know your opinion."

"Duce, would it not be best to form a block around yourself and the pennant of the Fasci, and await, weapons in hand, the enemy? There are so many of us, loyal, armed . . ."

"Certainly, that would be the most desirable end. . . but it is not always possible to do what we want. There are ongoing negotiations. Cardinal Schuster is acting as intermediary. Not a single drop of blood will be shed."

Actually, he said "I have been assured that not a single drop of blood will be shed."

"A transfer of power. For the government, a move to Valtellina, where Onori is preparing our quarters. We too will have to go to the mountains for a while."

I dared to interrupt:

"Do you trust the Cardinal, Duce?"

Mussolini raised his eyes and made a vague gesture with his hands.

"He's slimy. But I cannot doubt the words of a minister of God. This is the path I must take. Anyway, for me, it's over. I no longer have the right to demand sacrifices from Italians."

"But we want to join you in your fate . . ."

"You must obey. The life of Italy does not end this week or this month. Italy will rise again. It is a matter of years, or perhaps decades. But Italy will rise up, and it will be great again, as I myself had wanted."

After the briefest pause, he continued:

"So you will still be useful to the country. You will transmit the truth of our Idea to our children and grandchildren: the truth that has been falsified, defaced, camouflaged by too many bad, malicious actors, too many sell-outs, and a small portion of people are simply deluded."

Perhaps Mussolini did not say "too many." I had the impression that he only said "malicious actors and sell-outs." When he reread the lines that follow, he left a mark in the margin, and he made a gesture with his head to indicate that he was not too happy with the expression. Nevertheless, he left it there. His voice had that metallic tone that I had heard so often in his speeches. Then, more placidly, he continued:

> *"They say I made a mistake, that I should have had a better understanding of the men, that I lost my head, that I should never have declared war on France and England. They say that I should have withdrawn in 1938. They say that I should never have done this or that. It is easy to prophesize the past."*

I have never managed to recall the meaning of the mark in the margin here. Perhaps it means "I don't like it."

> *"History will have to consult my records to decide. But I have to say, by late May and early June 1940, if there was any criticism, it was to decry the scandal of a patently ridiculous, impolitic, bewildering neutrality. Germany had won. Not only would we have no reward; we would also, sooner or later, be invaded and crushed."*

Mussolini instructed me to indicate that the phrases he had underlined were what people were saying. With an even stronger stroke, he had underlined the words "Germany had won," along with what follows.

"And what is Mussolini doing? He's become soft. A golden opportunity like this will never come again.' This is what they were all saying, especially those who are now crying that we should have remained neutral and that only my megalomania, my lust for power, my weakness with Hitler, had brought the war. The truth is that there was no pressure from Hitler. Hitler had already won on the continent. He had no need for us. But we could not remain neutral if we wanted to maintain our position of parity with Germany, which we had maintained up to that point. The pacts with Hitler were exceedingly clear. I had and still have the utmost respect for him. You have to distinguish between Hitler and some of his men who tend to be more visible."

To these considerations, Mussolini added more. This, for example: "I was always speaking with the Führer about arrangements for Europe and Africa. There were no differences of opinion. Already during the negotiations over South Tyrol—an undeniable validation of his honest and sympathetic intentions—the Führer had demonstrated his goodwill and understanding. Europe would have been organized like so:"

"Europe divided into two large zones of influence: German influence in the north and north-east, Italian influence in the south, south-east, and south-west. More than one hundred years for the realization of this monumental plan. But one hundred years of peace and well-being. Was it wrong for me to greet a solution of this kind, of such scope, with hope and love? With one hundred years of fascist education and material wellbeing, the

Italian People would be able to attain a power in number and spirit to effectively counterbalance the overwhelming power of present-day Germany. A force of 300,000,000 Europeans, true Europeans—because I refuse to call those Balkan agglomerations true Europeans, or the people of certain areas of Russia, and those around the Vistola—a material and spiritual force to maneuver against the eventual enemy of Asia and America. Only an Axis victory would have given us the right to claim our share of the goods of this earth, of those goods that are held by a few greedy hands, and are the cause of all evil, of all the suffering, and of all the wars. The victory of the so-called Allied Powers will give the world a peace that is only ephemeral and illusory. For this reason, you, my faithful, must survive and keep the faith in your hearts. The world, when I am gone, will still need the Idea that was and will be the most audacious, the most original, and the most Mediterranean and European of all ideas. I was not bluffing when I declared that the Fascist Idea will be the Idea of the twentieth century. Whether it happens to be eclipsed for a few years or even a decade matters not. A combination of events and the weaknesses of men are what is causing today's eclipse. But there is no turning back. History will prove me right."

Here, Mussolini went quiet. He shook his head a few times as if to chase away some disturbing thought. Two days later, when I brought him the manuscript, at the point where he had spoken of a force of 300,000,000 Europeans, "real Europeans," he used his pencil to note a certain distance. He told me I had forgotten many important things. Today I can remember everything clearly.

Mussolini spoke of the position he took in 1933–34, up to the Stresa talks (April 1935). He confirmed that his actions were not entirely understood, and much less followed, by England and France. And he added:

"We were the only ones opposed to Germany's first expansionist efforts. I sent divisions to Brennero, but no cabinet in Europe would support me. Preventing Germany from disrupting the continental equilibrium, but at the same time allowing for the revision of the treaties; agreeing to a general adjustment of the borders, in a way that would satisfy Germany where it was justified in its claims, and initiating a restitution of its colonies: this is what would have prevented the war. A boiler needs a valve to keep working; hermetically seal it, and it explodes. Mussolini wanted peace, and was blocked."

After a brief silence, I dared to ask him:

"You said that the eventual victory of our enemies cannot bring lasting peace. In their propaganda they say. . ."
"Their propaganda is undoubtedly very effective. They have managed to convince everyone. I myself, at times. . ."

Mussolini underlined the phrase "I myself, at times. . ." and smiled. He put down his pencil and lifted his hands to his temples a few times. Then, speaking slowly, separating out the syllables, he added:

"Whatever they say is the truth. I have asked myself the reason for this form of collective inebriation. Do you know what I concluded?" He raised his head and stared at me. Then he continued: "I concluded that I had overestimated the intelligence of the masses. In the dialogues that I have so often had with the multitudes, I was convinced that the cries that followed my questions were a sign of consciousness, of comprehension, of evolution. Instead, it was collective hysteria."

"But the worst thing is that our enemies have managed to get the proletariat, the poor, the neediest, to rally heart and soul behind those who starve them, the plutocrats of big capital."

Mussolini marked these lines forcefully. I am sure I failed to properly record all of his thoughts. He said to me: "You have not said everything. You have shrunk down my ideas. We will talk about it again." But there was neither the time nor the means to discuss it further. A few days later, it was Dongo, the execution, Piazzale Loreto.

He said to me:

"Allied victory will roll back the front line of social demands. Russia? Russian State Capitalism (I believe it is superfluous to insist on the word "bolshevism") is the most advanced and the least socialist form of a hybrid capitalism, which can only be maintained in Russia, upheld by ignorance, fatalism, and stories of Cossacks who swapped the knout for the machine gun. Russian capitalism will inevitably and fatally clash with Anglo-Saxon capitalism. Only then will the Italian people have a

chance to rise up and prevail. The man who will have to play the
trump card. . ."

"That would be you, Duce. . ."

". . . will be a young man. I will be gone. Wait a few years for the
storms to pass. A pure young man shall rise: a leader who must
stir up the ideas of Fascism. Collaboration, not class struggle;
Labor Charter and socialism; sacredness of property, so long as
it does not become an insult to poverty; care and protection of
the workers, especially the old and invalid; care and protection
of mothers and infancy."

Mussolini wanted to underline these programmatic phrases. He clarified: "honor the father and the mother." He put down his pencil, indicated the corrections on the manuscript, and raised a hand to his face. Then, after a moment of silence, he added: "Sometimes you go back in time. It is great, after all: the nostalgia for the secure warmth of the maternal bosom." Then he continued:

"Fraternal assistance for the needy; morality in all fields;
struggle against ignorance, and against servility to the
powerful; reinforcement, if there is still time, of autarchy, our
unique hope until that utopian day when the raw materials that
God has given to the world can be shared among all peoples;
exaltation of the spirit of pride in being Italian; deep education,
not superficial, as has unfortunately been the case, due to the
turn of events rather than any ideological deficiency. There will
come a youth who will find our postulates of 1919 and those of
Verona of 1943 fresh and audacious and worthy of being

followed. The eyes of the people will then be open, and they themselves will decree the triumph of those ideas: ideas that too many interested parties never wanted to be understood and appreciated by the people, who believed that these ideas were opposed to them, to their moral and material interests . . ."

Here, too, Mussolini found that I had not recorded all that he had expressed. At the point where he talks about the utopian sharing of raw materials among the peoples of the earth, he corrected a glaring error. I blushed. He noticed this and smiled. Then he said:

"When you reproach yourself for having made a mistake, tell yourself that Mussolini makes twelve mistakes a day!"

Then he continued:

"We have had eighteen centuries of invasions and wretchedness, of declining birth rates and servitude, of internecine strife and ignorance, and, more than anything else, destitution and malnutrition. Twenty years of Fascism and seventy years of independence were not enough to give to the soul of every Italian the required force to overcome the crisis and understand the truth. The exceptions, magnificent and numerous, do not count. This crisis, which began in 1939, was not overcome by the Italian people. They will rise again, but convalescence will be long and sorrowful, and there will be consequences. I am like the great clinician who could not develop the right cure . . ."

Here I had written "diagnosis," which Mussolini changed to "cure." He thought for a moment, then added: "Diagnosis was correct!" He looked at me and said: "Let's add some other considerations . . ."

"... and who no longer has the trust of the important patient's family. Many other doctors rush to succeed me. Many are already known for their ineptitude; others are simply impudent or thirsty for profit. The new doctor still has to appear. And when he rises, he will have to take my formulas. He will simply have to know how to apply them better."
An accuser of Admiral Persano, asked what wrong the Admiral had done, responded: 'that of having lost.'
Like me. I have so much evidence here of how I tried, with all my might, to prevent the war, that I can be at perfect peace with the judgement of posterity and the conclusions of history."

When he said "I have so much evidence here" he indicated a large leather bag. I believe, of the three, it was the yellow one. Then he tapped a wooden case.

"I do not know if Churchill is, like me, serene and at peace. Remember: we frightened the world of big businessmen and speculators. They did not want us to be given a chance to live. If events of this war had been favorable to the Axis, I would have proposed world socialization to the Führer."

Mussolini gently smiled when he talked of his serenity and tranquility. He smiled once more when he referred to Churchill. The smile changed to a grimace of contempt as he spoke of businessmen and speculators.

> *"World socialization, and therefore: borders that are exclusively historical in character; abolition of every customs house; free trade between every country, regulated by an international convention; a single currency, and, consequently, common ownership of the world's gold, as well as raw materials, distributed according to the needs of each country; real and radical abolition of every armament. Colonies: those already developed become independent states; the others are distributed among the most appropriate countries according to density of population, or other criteria, for the purpose of colonizing and civilizing; freedom of thought, speech, and writing, regulated within certain limits: morality, first and foremost, has its rights."*

More precisely, Mussolini said: "Freedom of thought, speech, and the press? Yes, but regulated and moderated within reasonable limits. Without which, there would be anarchy and licence. And remember, above all, morality must have its rights."

> *"Every religion utterly free to propagandize: we are the first, the only, to restore prestige, decorum, freedom, and authority to the Catholic Church. Now we are witnessing an extraordinary spectacle: the same Church allied with its most bitter enemies."*

Mussolini initially said "to the Church," before adding "Catholic." He explained: "The Catholic Church does not want another power in Rome. The Church prefers weak adversaries to strong friends. Having an adversary to fight, which in the end cannot frighten it, and enables it to furnish the arguments with which to revive the faith, is undoubtedly an advantage." He clasped his hands and continued: "Skilled, refined diplomacy. But, at times, it is immensely damaging to engage in excessive cunning. With the fall of Fascism, the Catholic Church will find itself once again facing all kinds of enemies: old and new enemies. And it has cooperated in bringing down one of its only true, sincere defenders."

"In the south, in the so-called liberated zones, the dirty work of anti-clericalism is back in full swing. Compared to the publications of recent times, L'Asino was nothing but a provincial bulletin.[59] In this domain too, the same men who shut their eyes today will be unanimous in deploring their madness and bad faith. If victory had been ours, I would have offered this program to the world, and once again, it would be Rome to bring light to humanity."

At this point, Mussolini went quiet. He rose to his feet and approached the window. I had tried to make my notes as exact as possible, though I could barely keep up with his words, especially when the heat of his discourse made him hasten the velocity of expression. The pages now numbered more than thirty. Finally, Mussolini stepped back from the window. He turned to me once more and continued:

---

[59] [TN.] L'Asino (1892–1925) was a satirical magazine known for its anti-clericalism.

"They told me I should not have accepted, after Badoglio's armistice and my liberation, the position of leader of the state and government of the Social Republic. I should have retired to Switzerland, or to a state in South America. Had I not learned my lesson on July 25th? Was it my lust for power? Now I ask: should I really have kept my distance?"

In the copy of the manuscript that I presented to him the following day, Mussolini underlined the questions.

"I was physically unwell. I might have asked for at least a rest period. I would have seen events unfold. But what would have happened?

"The Germans were our allies. The alliance was signed, and reciprocal loyalty was sworn a thousand times, through the good times and the bad. The Germans, whatever error they may have committed, had, on September 8th, every right to feel and count themselves betrayed.

The 'traitors' of 1914 were the same as those of 1943. They had the right to behave like absolute masters. They would have certainly nominated their occupying military government. And what would have happened? Scorched earth. Famine, mass deportations, abductions, occupation currency,[60] forced labor. Our industry, our artistic, industrial, and personal values, would all be spoils of war.

---

[60] [TN.] The AM-Lira (Allied-Military Currency) was introduced by the Allied Military Government for Occupied Territories after the Allied landing in Sicily in 1943.

I have reflected on this at length. I decided by obeying the love I have for this divine land, which is worthy of adoration. I had, precisely, the conviction to sign my own death sentence. I was no longer important. I had to save as many lives and assets as possible; I had to search once more for some way to do good for the people of Italy. And the occupation currency, the war marks, which were already in circulation, were, by my will, withdrawn. I imposed myself.[61] I bellowed. Today we would have billions of notes, which would only have been good for the fire. And in the south the legal governors have accepted the occupation currency. Our lira has practically no value there anymore. The so-called liberated zones are now regaled with horrendous inflation. When they arrive in the north,[62] the north that the Social Republic has governed despite bombardments, roadblocks, partisan and rebel operations; despite the shortage of food and fuel; in this north where the bread still costs what it cost eighteen months ago, and where you can eat at the Mense del Popolo for eight lira; when they arrive to liberate the north, they will bring, along with other evils, inflation. The price of bread will jump to one hundred lira per kilo, and everything will be in proportion . . ."

I believe that here I rendered Mussolini's thinking accurately enough, because the next day, rereading these pages, he signaled his approval with frequent nods of his head.

---

[61] [TN.] This sentence is missing in RC.
[62] [TN.] Error in RC: "when we arrive."

"I imposed myself and had men who obeyed me. Only the required minimum of money was printed. I did, however, authorize the banks to issue cashier's checks; those checks that receive so much criticism. They cannot be hoarded: that is their importance. The currency is in demand and buys credit; yield on government bonds is at 120, and we need to hit the brakes to prevent another increase. All this, I have accomplished. I prevented machinery from being taken to Bavaria. I worked to ensure the return of thousands of deported soldiers and workers. On this point, too, let me be clear: my figures are indisputable. More than 360,000 workers volunteered to work in Germany, and for four years they sent billions to their families. Another 320,000 workers were enlisted by the Todt.[63] From Germany, more than 400,000 soldiers and officers returned, because they were prisoners, because of personal preference, or, in some of the more painful cases, because of my own personal interest.

I prevented many executions by firing squad, even when they were justified. I tried, with three decrees of amnesty and pardon, to slow as much as possible the repressive actions that the German Command required in order to ensure that their fighters were protected and secure. I had provisions distributed to the poor, without ever inquiring about the opinions of a single one of those millions of people. I tried to save what could be saved. Up until now, order has been maintained: in work, in transport, in the cities.

---

[63] [TN.] The Todt (1933–1945) was a National Socialist civil and military engineering organization responsible for many engineering projects in Germany and occupied territories.

There are rebels. They are numerous. But, apart from a portion of people who have been deceived, the bulk is composed of runaways, deserters, labor camp escapees, and prisoners. The allies know this perfectly well, but they also know that these formations are extremely useful for their war efforts. With liberation, it will be like what happened in Greece. In your paper you have rightly highlighted the desperate transmissions of the Greek partisans who struggle against the English liberators."

A clandestine radio transmission by the Greek partisans fighting against the British had been intercepted. I put the story in the paper, and had a few thousand copies distributed in the partisan zones.

"Faced with a situation that I saw with tragic precision, was I supposed to desert my position of responsibility? Just read the papers from the south: 'Mussolini, prisoner of the Germans,' 'Mussolini has lost his mind,' 'Mussolini is ill,' 'Mussolini with his mistress,' 'Mussolini has progressive paralysis,' 'Mussolini has fled to Brazil.'"

Mussolini showed me the clippings. He read the titles aloud. Each time, after articulating the syllables of each title, he raised his eyes to see my reaction. Then he tightened his fist and pounded the table.

"Instead I am here, at my post, where the victors will find me. I will also be working in Valtellina. I will try to ensure that the world knows the absolute and undeniable truth of how the events of the last five years unfolded. There is but a single truth."

"But is there still hope? Are there secret weapons?"

"There are. If that attack on Hitler last summer had not happened, there would be time to put these weapons to use. In Germany too, betrayal has brought ruin, not for the party, but for the Fatherland."

More precisely, Mussolini said: "there are: it would be ridiculous and unforgivable to bluff." And when he said the word "betrayal" he exclaimed: "But we were always, and will always be loyal." He then placed his hand on my shoulder and said with sadness: "So many oaths! So many pledges of loyalty and dedication! Only now do I see who was truly loyal, who was truly fascist! It was you guys, always the same, loyal through the good times and the bad. It was easy to glorify people in 1938! I have so many records of people who in the end did nothing for me. At the first sight of the tempest, they withdrew to see how things would unfold. Then they joined the other side. What a sorry state of affairs. But what comfort, in the end, to see that there are people who are pure, true, and sincere. To betray the idea. . . to betray me. . . but to betray the Fatherland!" Then, speaking once more about secret weapons, he declared:

"Those famously destructive bombs are being readied. Just a few days ago, I received a detailed update. Perhaps Hitler only wants to strike when he knows the blow will be decisive. It appears there are three of these formidably effective bombs. The construction of each is a tremendously long and complicated process. Romania's betrayal has also had an impact, since the gas shortage was the deciding factor in the loss of air

supremacy. Twenty or thirty thousand aircraft grounded or destroyed. Lack of fuel. The most terrible of tragedies."

"Duce, do you think the English and Americans will simply watch as the Russians enter the heart of Europe? Will it not be possible to take a stand . . . ?"

"The armored cars entering East Prussia are American brand."

At this point, Mussolini wanted to clarify that he did not think it was possible to hope for any turnaround at the front. He also said: "Perhaps Hitler is deceived." Then he added: "And yet, there would still be time, if . . ." He arched his eyebrows, made a broad gesture with his hands, as if trying to make me understand: "Anything is possible." Then he resumed:

"The mission of the allies is to destroy the Axis. Then . . ."

"Then?"

"I told you. A third world war will break out: capitalist democracies against capitalist bolshevism. Only our victory would have given the world peace with justice. They always reproached me for the tyrannical form of discipline I imposed on Italians. How they'll regret it. And it will have to return, if Italians want to be a people again, instead of an agglomeration of slaves. And Italians will want it, and demand it. They will drive out the false shepherds from the people, the wicked little men subservient to foreign interests. They will bring flowers to the tombs of the martyrs, to the tombs of those fallen for an idea that will be the light and the hope of the world. They will say,

then, without flattery, and without falsity: 'Mussolini was right.'"

At this point, Mussolini took the pages where he had taken notes.

"You won't write an article. Take from these notes what I have told you. Bring me the manuscript in the morning two days from now. If I have the time, we will resume our work in a few days."

I said to Il Duce that in the hall there was my editor-in-chief, who had been the editor of a weekly magazine in Brescia. Mussolini had someone call him. We remained there for another ten minutes. That night—the 21st-22nd of April—I finished preparing these notes, which I would bring to Il Duce the next day. Due to lack of paper, I had to write the last four pages on the back of the first four.

I hope I have accurately interpreted the thoughts of Il Duce.

Viva Mussolini!

Viva the Social Republic!

Viva Fascism!

When dictation was complete, Editor-in-Chief Second Lieutenant Lucarini entered.

Mussolini talked with us, laughing and joking for about fifteen minutes. When we exited into the hall, we were surrounded by party officials and comrades. Vittorio Mussolini wanted to see the photograph. Mezzasoma said:

"It's extremely rare for him to write such dedications."

Then I got to work. I worked all night on the newspaper. The edition of April 21st, however, was no longer going to be published. The following night I put the notes in order. I worked as much as I could. Three air raid sirens; three times the lights went out. The morning of April 22nd, at 11:00, I returned to the Prefecture. Mussolini was out.

I returned at 12:40. I crossed the hall at a rapid pace. He responded with a tired air to our greetings. When he reached the threshold of his room, he turned and signaled for me to wait.

Barracu, after about ten minutes, brought me in. He was eating. They had brought a tray with a soup tureen. He sipped a few spoonfuls of soup, then ate some green leaves, a small piece of boiled meat, two potatoes, and a boiled carrot. Then an apple. He drank two fingers of mineral water. Then he turned to me and said: "Show me your work."

He drew back from the pages. He read attentively, slowly. His face had visible traces of tiredness. Though it was only forty-eight hours since I last saw him, he seemed to have aged. He made corrections and many marks, as is evident from the manuscript. When he finished, he said to me:

"Alright. Maybe we will see each other again in a few days. If something should happen, show no one this text. If the collapse should occur, keep it hidden for three years. Then go ahead, according to circumstances and your criteria. Now go."

I saluted without managing to say a word.

He smiled at me and made a gesture of goodbye.

I exited the Prefecture with my mind in turmoil.

I would never see him again.

Milan,

April 22nd, 1945